+HB871 .S65 1980+

50664000137801
Spengler, Joseph Joh/Declining populatio
HB871 .S65 1980 C.1 STACKS 1980

HB 871 S65 1980

Spengler, Joseph John, 1902–

Declining population growth revisited

DATE DUE

COLLEGE FOR HUMAN SERVICES
LIBRARY
345 HUDSON STREET
NEW YORK, N.Y. 10014

DECLINING POPULATION GROWTH REVISITED

JOSEPH J. SPENGLER

GREENWOOD PRESS, PUBLISHERS
WESTPORT, CONNECTICUT

Library of Congress Cataloging in Publication Data

Spengler, Joseph John, 1902-
  Declining population growth revisited.

  Reprint of the ed. published by Carolina Population
Center, Chapel Hill, N.C., which was issued as no. 14
of the Center's Monograph.
  Bibliography: p.
  1. Population. 2. Economic development.
I. Title. II. Series: Carolina Population Center.
Monograph ; 14.
[HB871.S65 1980]   304.6'2   80-23714
ISBN 0-313-22621-0 (lib. bdg.)

© Carolina Population Center 1971

Carolina Population Center, Monograph 14.

Reprinted with the permission of The Carolina Population
Center, The University of North Carolina.

Reprinted in 1980 by Greenwood Press
A division of Congressional Information Service, Inc.
88 Post Road West, Westport, Connecticut 06881

Printed in the United States of America

10 9 8 7 6 5 4 3 2 1

THE AUTHOR

Joseph J. Spengler, who holds the James B. Duke professorship of economics and is director of the training program in demography and ecology at Duke University as well as a faculty associate of the Carolina Population Center, is author or co-author of eleven books and has contributed chapters to 56 others, including population volumes edited by Philip Hauser, Kingsley Davis, and Ronald Freedman. Approximately half of his professional writing has had strong pertinence to population. He has been president of the Population Association of America, the American Economic Association, and the Southern Economic Association; vice-president of the Economic History Association and the American Association for Advancement of Science; has been named a fellow of a half-dozen scholarly societies; has been a member of the Social Science Research Council and the National Research Council Division of Behavioral Sciences, as well as consultant to corporations, government agencies, the Ford Foundation, and the United Nations.

LIST OF TABLES

TABLE 1 *Age Composition, 1930-1990* 29

TABLE 2 *Female Age Composition, 1965-2060* 30

TABLE 3 *Projected Population, 1970-2037* 32

TABLE 4 *Age Structure, 1970-2020* 33

TABLE 5 *Population Growth, by Age Group, 1970-2020* 35

TABLE 6 *Age Composition of Stationary Population* 41

TABLE 7 *Age Composition of Male Growing and Stationary Populations* 46

DECLINING POPULATION GROWTH REVISITED

An author attempting to understand a phenomenon normally felt as deplorable... frequently ends up by identifying with it and turning explanation into apology and apology into eulogy.
A. O. Hirschman, *Journeys Toward Progress*
Change is, however, not "natural," not normal, much less ubiquitous and constant. Fixity is.
R. A. Nisbet, *Social Change and History*

Popular discussion and perhaps also academic discussion of implications of the population prospect may take on Hegelian guise over the next twenty-five or more years. Belief in the continuation of population growth, powerful since the day of Malthus, may be said always to have undergirded economic and other expectations and policy. Only in the 1930's did fear of cessation of population growth temporarily offset this belief. For the past several decades, however, it has been virtually taken for granted that the population of the conterminous United States, now about 205 million as expected, will number 300 or more million by the year 2000 and still be growing around one percent per year.

This supposition is now being called into question. For statistical reasons given below, it is now expected that as of the year 2000 our population will remain some millions short of 300. Meanwhile contraceptive techniques will be improving and knowledge of them virtually universally diffused, access to abortion will become even easier, and the Zero-Rate-of-Population-Growth movement will be emphasizing the need to halt population growth. This combination of forces, some now believe, could depress fertility below the long-run replacement level.

It is to be expected that as knowledge spreads of continuing decline in the rate of population growth as well as of the prospective advent of a stationary population, considerable concern if not also alarm will develop in the business and other communities. Such concern has already been manifested in overpopulated Japan[1] where also population growth appears to be grinding to a halt. After all, we now live in a growth-stressing and growth-oriented age and society, one making an unquestionable virtue of growth. This view differs from that which led many economists, following J. S. Mill, to stress the advantages of a stationary state, at least in a world dominated by the Anglo-Saxon. In recent times, numerophiliacs sometimes have professed to see no relation between population growth and growth of G.N.P. per head.

Given alarm at the advent of a stationary population, perhaps accompanied by demands for fertility-stimulating measures, counterargument may be anticipated, given the now increasingly widespread acceptance of the view that population growth is no longer contributive to average welfare.

Should alarm at the advent of a population growing very slowly if at all generate arguments that population growth as well as economic growth is good and to be encouraged, the antithesis of these views will surely find expression. This likelihood is all the greater now that various so-called welfare measures are being advocated, even by conservatives, in nearly complete disregard of the stimulus thereby given to multiplication, both in general and among those least able to provide a satisfactory socioeconomic environment for children.

In what follows I examine some effects of the advent of a decline in the rate of population growth and of its descent to zero. Before examining and assessing the current and the prospective situation, however, I review in Section I man's past manifestation of concern at the threat of a decline in numbers. In Sections II and III the impact of a decline in the rate of population growth upon the rate of growth of the demand for non-durable and durable products, respectively, is examined, together with how this impact is cushioned. Section IV is ancillary to Sections II and III in that it deals with whether the behavior of laws of returns necessitates modification of the analysis in II and III. Implications of changes in age composition are treated in Section V, and of the advent of a stationary state and stationary economy in Sections VI and VII.

---

1. E.g., on Japan see P. M. Boffey, "Japan: A Crowded Nation Wants to Boost Its Birthrate," *Science* 167 (February 13, 1970): 960-62.

Conclusions follow. In the last three sections stress is placed upon the importance of planning how to adapt to zero or very low growth rates rather than upon attempting to halt the advent of a stationary population.

I shall not be dealing with growth theory as such other than in several references to the laws of returns in Section IV. Nor is attention devoted to the optimizing of population growth and/or size. The issues are important, however, involving as they do how to proceed most efficiently under given conditions to a given point, together with considerations of choice between generations and between more or less population growth.

I. PAST MANIFESTATIONS OF CONCERN

Today's economies differ remarkably from those of two centuries ago and significantly from those of around 1900 and even from those of the 1930's. Not only is the role of the state much greater even in non-centralized economies. The growth of today's economy also depends far more upon technical progress than in the past, with capital formation contributing in much greater measure than formerly to the satisfaction of public and domestic requirements and to the incorporation and mobilization of invention and innovation. The contribution of growth of the working population to economic growth is much less important today than formerly, particularly if labor as such is distinguished from the skill embodied in labor through education. One is almost tempted to say, therefore, that today alarm at decline in the rate of population arises from fear that there will be too few consumers rather than from fear that the labor force will be growing too slowly.

Despite these changes and the emerging of new emphases in modern states, it is likely that, because of increase in alarm at the slowness with which numbers are increasing, time-hallowed bugaboos respecting demographic non-growth may be disinterred and unwise if not witless natality-favoring measures may be put forward. Review of past manifestations of concern may not be amiss.

Until the eighteenth century, despite periodic intensification of population pressure, publicists generally favored population growth. William Godwin observed correctly in 1820, in his reply to Malthus,[2] that statesmen had generally been interested in en-

---

2. *Of Population* (London, 1820), pp. 52, 88-89, 103, 108-9.

couraging population growth, at least until Malthus' views had become ascendant.[3] Thereafter, not until the mid-nineteenth century was much concern manifested in a European country, France, at the slowness of its population growth, concern that did not, however, give rise to a well-rounded pro-natalist policy until the eve of World War II.[4] French concern rested mainly on political and military considerations. It had the support, however, of French industrialists who wanted "cheap" labor, much as did American industrialists when, after World War I, they opposed control of immigration into the United States.

Although Edwin Cannan, in 1895, forecast the cessation of England's population growth, a syndrome of forces favorable to pro-natalist policy did not emerge until in the 1930's. Right after World War I, J. M. Keynes pointed to population pressure as a factor contributing to the occurrence of this war, and soon after that Malthus' geometrical ratio was rediscovered by a number of writers.[5] In the late 1920's, the careful work of L. I. Dublin and A. J. Lotka revealed that the true rate of natural increase in the United States was much below the crude rate, and R. R. Kuczynski's studies revealed a similar disparity in Northern and Western Europe.[6] Continuation of the decline of crude natality, under the double impact of the Great Depression and longer-run

---

3. See my *French Predecessors of Malthus* (Durham: Duke University Press, 1942), translated as "Economie et population. Les doctrines francaises avant 1800" and including an appendix by Alfred Sauvy, Paris, I.N.E.D., 1954; also my "Mercantilist and Physiocratic Growth Theory," in B. F. Hoselitz, ed., *Theories of Economic Growth* (Glencoe: Free Press, 1960); D. V. Glass, *Population Policies and Movements in Europe* (Oxford: Oxford University Press, 1940); C. E. Strangeland, *Pre-Malthusian Doctrines of Population* (New York: Columbia University Press, 1904).

4. On the emergence of this concern see my *France Faces Depopulation* (Durham: Duke University Press, 1938); and on the policies, Cicely Watson, "Population Policy in France: Family Allowances and Other Benefits," *Population Studies* 7 (1953-54): 263-86; 8 (1954-55): 46-73, and J. Doublet, "Family Allowances in France," *ibid.* 2 (1948-49): 219-39; also Cicely Watson, "Birth Control and Abortion in France Since 1939," *ibid.* 5 (1951-52): 261-86, and "Housing Policy and Population Problems in France," *ibid.* 7 (1953-54): 14-15. See also running accounts in *Population*. Concern at low natality was manifest in New England in the last third of the nineteenth century. See my "Notes on Abortion, Birth Control, and Medical and Sociological Interpretations of the Birth Rate in Nineteenth Century America," *Marriage Hygiene* 2 (1935-36): 43-53, 158-59, 288-300. Malthusianism was not yet favored in America. See Edmond Cocks, "The Malthusian Theory in Pre-Civil War America," *Population Studies* 20 (1966-67): 343-63,

5. See Keynes, *The Economic Consequences of the Peace* (New York: Harcourt, Brace, and Howe, 1920), and A. B. Wolfe's detailed account in "The Population Problem Since the World War," *Journal of Political Economy* 36 (1928): 529-59, 662-85; 37 (1929): 87-120. Edwin Cannan's forecast is reprinted in his *Economic Scares* (London: P. S. King & Son, 1933), pp. 108ff., also 125ff.

6. L. I. Dublin and A. J. Lotka, "On the True Rate of Natural Increase as Exemplified by the Population of the United States," *Journal of the American Statistical Association* 20 (September, 1925): 305-39; R. R. Kuczynski, *The Balance of Births and Deaths* (New York: Macmillan, 1928), and *The Measurement of Population Growth* (New York: Oxford University Press, 1936).

socioeconomic changes, seemed to foretoken the early advent of a stationary if not a declining population.[7] In military-oriented Italy and Germany, a pro-natalist policy came into existence.[8] In the United States, intensification of the Great Depression was associated with decline in both the rate of natural increase and the demand for capital supposedly resulting.[9] Elsewhere proponents of a "Welfare State" found in the alleged need for pro-natalist measures and their adoption a means to the acceleration of the enactment of broad welfare programs.[10]

A considerable literature relating to supposed economic effects of a decline in the rate of population growth appeared in the 1930's. Receiving most emphasis—as a result of the appearance of Keynes's *General Theory* in 1936—was the supposed need to find investment outlets to replace those—about one-half of all investment—formerly supplied by the growth and spread of population;[11] for response to changes in the interest rate was deemed inadequate to maintain balance between savings and offsets to savings at or near an economy's full-employment level.[12] As a result of the slowing down of population growth, cyclical tendencies, fed through the accelerator principle, and consequently greater fluctuation in capital requirements than in consumption, would be intensified. So great was the interest in imbalance between ex ante savings and ex ante investment that other causes of unemployment tended to be neglected. Concern was expressed also lest labor mobility be reduced and result in sub-optimal distribution of the labor force among industries and occupations. Increase in the relative number of older persons might convert administrative structures of economies into gerontocracies, it was said, as well as reduce average output under

---

7. E.g., see Warren Thompson and P. K. Whelpton, *Population Trends in The United States* (New York: McGraw-Hill, 1933); Enid Charles, *The Twilight of Parenthood* (New York: Norton, 1934); Kuczynski, *The Balance of Births and Deaths;* Lancelot Hogben, ed., *Political Arithmetic* (New York: Macmillan, 1938), chap. 24. For a critique of the projections see J. S. Davis, *The Population Upsurge in the United States,* War-Peace Pamphlet No. 12, Stanford (Calif.) Food Research Institute, December, 1949.

8. E.g., see D. V. Glass, *Population Policies and Movements in Europe,* and *The Struggle for Population* (Oxford: Oxford University Press, 1936).

9. E.g., see A. H. Hansen, *Fiscal Policy and Business Cycles* (New York: Norton, 1941), and "Economic Progress and Declining Population," *American Economic Review* 39 (March, 1939): 1-15; also J. M. Keynes, "Some Consequences of a Declining Population," *Eugenics Review* 29 (1937): 13-17; and Ben Higgins, "The Theory of Increasing Unemployment," *Economic Journal* 60 (June, 1950): 255-74.

10. E.g., see Alva Myrdal, *Nation and Family* (New York: Harper & Brothers, 1941).

11. Something like half of all physical capital outlay had been upon population growth. On population growth and capital requirements see Simon Kuznets, *Capital in the American Economy* (Princeton: Princeton University Press, 1961), chap. 7.

12. That the American economy was operating at below capacity was stressed also in a series of studies carried on at the Brookings Institution. E.g., see H. G. Moulton, *Income and Economic Progress* (Washington, D.C.: The Brookings Institution, 1935).

given technological conditions and price structures. Attention was devoted also to family-allowance and other arrangements suited to stimulate natality.[13] Little or no reference was made to possible implications of differences between the rates of population growth in developed countries and those in underdeveloped countries. The latter remained below one percent until in the 1920's and (with the exception of periods when the advanced countries were at war) did not rise above those of the advanced countries until in the 1930's, and not notably until in and after the 1950's. In contrast, the rate of growth in today's underdeveloped world is about 2.5 times that in the developed world (currently in the neighborhood of one percent).

The outbreak of World War II diverted attention from the threat of population decline and so also did the resulting destruction and/or absorption of capital. This diversion continued into the 1950's as a result of the post-war upsurge of natality, natural increase, and the need for goods and services oriented to children. Meanwhile and subsequently, the so-called doctrine of "economic maturity" was called into question,[14] and other causes of unemployment were noted (e.g., structural causes, excessive labor cost).[15] At the same time it was pointed out that though ex ante investment tended to exceed ex ante savings and produce inflation in underdeveloped countries, there could also be great unemployment in overpopulated poor countries characterized by inequality and capital shortage, especially if wages were propped up uneconomically in the alleged name of justice.[16] It was also implied that the demand for labor in an advanced country could

---

13. Watson, "Population Policy in France: Family Allowances and Other Benefits"; Myrdal, *Nation and Family*. Representative of the literature are W. B. Reddaway, *The Economics of a Declining Population* (London: George Allen and Unwin, 1939); Hans Neisser, "The Economics of a Stationary Population," *Social Research* 11 (November, 1944): 470-90; Gunnar Myrdal, *Population; A Problem for Democracy* (Cambridge: Harvard University Press, 1940); papers in J. J. Spengler and Otis Dudley Duncan, eds., *Population Theory and Policy* (Glencoe: Free Press, 1956), esp. pp. 234-304, and *Demographic Analysis* (Glencoe: Free Press, 1956), esp. pp. 439-77, 492-517. See also Lionel Robbins, "Notes on Some Probable Consequences of the Advent of a Stationary Population in Great Britain," *Economica* 9 (April, 1929): 71-82, and my "The Social and Economic Consequences of Cessation in Population Growth," *Proceedings of the Congresso International Per Gli Studi Sulla Popolazione* (1932), Rome, 1933, 9: 33-60.

14. E.g., see George Terborgh, *The Bogey of Economic Maturity* (Chicago: Machinery and Allied Products Institute, 1945); also D. S. Landes, *The Unbound Prometheus: Technological Change and Industrial Development in Western Europe from 1750 to the Present* (Cambridge: Cambridge University Press: 1969).

15. E.g, see J. M. Peterson and C. T. Stewart, Jr., *Employment Effects of Minimum Wage Rates* (Washington, D.C.: American Enterprise Institute, 1969).

16. E.g., see J. E. Meade, "Population Explosion, the Standard of Living and Social Conflict," *Economic Journal* 73 (June, 1967): 233-55. Even in Puerto Rico, despite heavy investment and emigration, unemployment has remained high because inputs complementary to labor have been in short supply.

and would prove excessive if budgetary constraints were ignored. For example, L. A. Lecht estimated that full achievement by the mid-1970's of 16 goals (which originated with President Eisenhower's Commission on National Goals and which ranged in subject from agriculture to extraterrestrial space) would "require an employed civilian labor force of more than 100 million–some 10 million more than are expected to be in the civilian labor force in 1975."[17]

Alarm at decline in the rate of population growth seems to be arising less from the decline as such than from failure of expectations based upon the assumption of a higher rate of growth than is in prospect.[18] The business community may be said to take an asymmetrical view of the impact of population growth. Emphasis is placed almost exclusively upon the contribution that population growth makes to the growth of demand; relatively little attention is paid to the contribution of increase in average income, the counterpart of increase in net national product per capita. Neglected is the fact that Gross National Product is one side of the coin and Gross Aggregate Demand is the other—that these two aggregates are equal to each other. The problem involved insofar as there is a problem is but an accentuation of an ever present problem in a modern economy, that of adjusting the composition of the Aggregate Supply of goods and services to the Aggregate Demand for goods and services.

At this point a brief examination of the gross population prospect is in order. The prospect may be expressed in terms of the crude birth rate (whose movement for the past 35 years has paralleled that of the general fertility rate), the crude rate of natural increase, and the overall rate of population growth. Other aspects will be noted in later sections. The rate of natural increase was 15.3 per 1,000 inhabitants in the 1950's, nearly double the 1935-39 rate, but it moved down in the 1960's as the birth rate declined, from 24.3 in 1959 to 17.7 in 1969, and natural increase fell to 8.1 per 1,000 in 1968-69. Net civilian immigration, running about 2 per 1,000 inhabitants in the 1960's, is keeping the crude

---

17. *Manpower Requirements for National Objectives in the 1970's,* prepared for the U.S. Dept. of Labor, Manpower Administration, by Leonard A. Lecht of the Center for Priority Analysis, National Planning Association, Washington, D.C., February, 1968, summary in chaps. 1, 8. See also A. J. Jaffe and Joseph Froomkin, *Technology and Jobs* (New York: Praeger, 1968).

18. E.g., see L. A. Mayer, "Why the U.S. Population Isn't Exploding," *Fortune* (April, 1967): 188ff., and "New Questions About the U.S. Population," *ibid.* (February, 1971): 80ff.; also citations in A. J. Coale, "Population Change and Demand...," in Coale, ed., *Demographic and Economic Change in Developed Countries* (Princeton: Princeton University Press, 1960), pp. 352-76, esp. pp. 356-57.

growth rate at around one percent, though the absolute number of births fell below four million after 1964.

Turning to the fertility assumptions underlying the two lowest of the four projections of several years ago, we find them based, respectively, on the supposition that completed fertility per woman would average 2.78 and 2.45 children, respectively, and that consequently population would approximate 308 and 283 million, respectively, figures now reduced to 301 and 281 millions. Given, as in the previous cases, an annual immigration of 400,000, and a completed fertility of 2.11, the nation's population would number 266 million in 2000. Without net immigration, this figure would approximate 250 million by 2000 and a stationary figure of 276 million by 2037. A completed fertility rate of 2.11 is compatible with the assumption that perhaps one birth in eight is unwanted. In January, 1969, it was probable that women then 25-29 would finally average about 2.8 children per woman, or about one-third more than the 2.13 required to replace the population, and thus sustain a rate of population growth of about one percent per year. Should fertility decline when women reached age 30 or more years the final figure would be below 2.8.[19]

The new projections suggest that the rate of population growth over the next 45 years will approximate one percent per year, or even less should most unwanted births be prevented and the fertility level move quickly toward the replacement level. Several years ago a long-run rate of growth of 1 3/8 percent per year was considered probable for the period 1966-2015. This rate was subject to some variation as would be a lower rate, since it is affected by changes in the relative number of women aged 19-34 years and by how newly married couples plan to distribute over time the number of births they prefer.

II. POPULATION MOVEMENTS AND DEMAND FOR NON-DURABLE PRODUCTS

In this and the next section I examine the impact of change in the rate of population growth upon the rate of growth of demand

---

19. In this paragraph I have drawn on Bureau of the Census, "Population Estimates," in *Current Population Reports,* Series P-25, No. 381, December 18, 1967, pp. 52, 67, No. 388, March 14, 1968, No. 448, August, 1970, and "Projections of the Number of Households and Families 1967 to 1985," No. 399, June 6, 1968; see also Series P-20, No. 203, July 6, 1970. See also Tomas Frejka, "Reflections on the Demographic Conditions Needed to Establish a U.S. Stationary Population Growth," *Population Studies* 22 (November, 1968): 379-97. About one birth in five or six is unwanted. L. Bumpass and C. F. Westoff, "The 'Perfect Contraceptive' Population," *Science* 169 (September 18, 1970): 1177-82.

for non-durable and durable goods, respectively. These are dealt with separately because they differ with respect to sensitivity to population growth. Attention will be focused upon categories of intersubstitutable goods, since the growth of demand for individual, particular goods is little influenced by change in the rate of growth of population. The findings of this and the next section relate to countries with conditions similar to those encountered in modern economies; they do not relate to undeveloped countries or to medieval economies where methods of production are primitive and average output increases little or not at all.[20]

Only passing reference is made to internal migration. It becomes significant in the context of the present analysis only insofar as (a) it is a function of the rate of population growth and (b) it makes total demand larger or smaller than it otherwise would have been. Point (b) is of little significance with respect to non-durables but it probably increases the overall demand for durables.

Analysis of the behavior of demand is complicated by the number of determinants that influence it in both the short and the long run. For the sake of expositive convenience we may put the short-run determinants in formula form and later proceed to examine longer-run determinants. We may write with Wold[21]

$$\log d = \log c + E \log i - e \log p + a \log x + b \log y + \ldots + g \log u.$$

---

20. W. C. Robinson points out that in medieval Europe growth of population did not necessarily give rise to increase in money income or purchasing power and hence to increase in demand. The medieval European situation does not, of course, correspond closely to those encountered in present-day underdeveloped countries, since the forces making for income increase in these countries are much more powerful than those encountered in medieval Europe, and requisite growth-facilitating mechanisms are present. See Robinson, "Money, Population, and Economic Change in Late Medieval Europe," *Economic History Review* 12 (August, 1959): 63-82, esp. pp. 68-70. Representative of today's relationships are those determined by Ben-Chich Liu, "The Relationships Among Population, Income, and Retail Sales in SMSA's, 1952-66," *Quarterly Review of Economics and Business* 10 (1970): 25-30. Population elasticity of demand for retail sales, automotive sales, and gas station sales are quite high, as a rule. *Ibid.*: 34-35.

21. On demand see H. O. Wold, *Demand Analysis* (New York: Wiley, 1953), esp. pp. 3ff.; H. S. Houthakker and L. D. Taylor, *Consumer Demand in the United States 1929-1970* (Cambridge: Harvard University Press, 1966), chap. 7 and pp. 1-2, 34-36, 173-74, 196-200. See also Coale, "Population Change and Demand...," pp. 352-76; A. C. Kelley, "Demographic Change and Economic Growth: Australia, 1861-1911," *Explorations in Entrepreneurial History* 5 (1968): 115-85; and "Demand Patterns, Demographic Change, and Economic Growth," *Quarterly Journal of Economics* 83 (February, 1969): 110-26; Charles Zwick, "Demographic Variation: Its Impact on Consumer Behavior," *Review of Economics and Statistics* 39 (November, 1957): 451-56. According to H. Anderson, population growth needs to be taken into account when forecasting short-run demand only when the demand function is of appropriate form. See his "Population Size and Demand," *Southern Economic Journal* 28 (October, 1961): 182-86; and cf. V. L. Bassie, "Relationship of Population Changes to Economic Prosperity," *Current Economic Comment* 20 (May, 1958): 33-38.

Here i is aggregate income, p is price, $x, y, \ldots, u$ are other factors which influence demand, and $E, e, a, b, \ldots, g$ are elasticities which may be treated as constants. Here log d designates the demand here and now for a particular good, the determinants of which are on the right hand side of the equation. The elasticities reveal how sensitive demand is to a change in any particular determinant. The value of the coefficient of elasticity, say e of price p, indicates the percentage change in demand that accompanies a one percent change in price. If this change is two percent, the value of e is 2 and thus indicates greater sensitivity to price change than would e = 1.0. In the longer run the values of some elasticities increase, since demanders are able, given time, to adjust their response more nicely to changes in price, income, etc. It is evident that demand d depends on many factors and so also must the rate of increase in demand of individuals. It is also evident that, as a rule, population growth contributes very little to growth of demand for *individual* products. It is essential, therefore, to group together into distinct categories goods which are highly substitutable for one another, for such categories are far more sensitive to population change than are individual goods.

The i in the above equation plays a major role in the analysis that follows; it designates aggregate income and is the product of population multiplied by average income. The rate of increase in income i approximates the sum of the rate of increase in population and the rate of increase in average income—that is P' + y' where P' and y' denote the respective rates of increase in population P and average income y.

Analysis of the impact of change in the rate of population growth requires one to allow for or to standardize for demographic and other concomitants of population change that may affect the response of demand to population growth. Accordingly, we rule out for the present changes in age and household composition by postulating a stable population in Sections II and III and treating age composition later on in Section V. A distinction is made between durable and non-durable goods, i.e., those whose embodied services are used up in less than one or two years, because the demand for the latter responds differently to change in rate of population growth than does demand for the former. It is also assumed in Sections II and III that average output does not increase as a result of population growth—in technical terms, that returns are constant, *not* increasing or decreasing. In Section IV the tenability of this assumption is discussed.

Occasional reference will be made to internal migration though it affects only where non-durables are consumed, not how much is consumed per capita. Internal migration would be important were we concerned with changes in local instead of national demand. For, whereas international migration does not usually greatly affect national rates of population growth, internal migration sometimes produces great variability in the rate of population growth at state, metropolitan, and regional levels. Net internal migration may remove a large fraction of an area's natural increase, or it may add as many people as does natural increase.[22] The volume of local migration may be influenced by the overall rate of population growth; it is affected by a variety of factors, among them the relative number of persons who are describable as migration-prone. This volume may also be affected by interregional differences in economic change, a kind of change to which a region may be more sensitive than a country is to changes in the conditions of international trade. Internal migration does not, however, suffice to eliminate all interregional differences.

Let us return now to the problem posed in the second paragraph in this section. It was there implied that population growth had little influence upon the demand for individual products. It becomes necessary, therefore, to distinguish specific, individual products from sets of individual products, each yielding indentical or nearly identical services and linked to other members of the same set by high cross-elasticities of demand (i.e., with similarly behaving demands). Change in the demand for an individual member of such a set is dominated in the longer run by technological change, changes in taste, the volatility of wants (associated with increase in the discretionary income and discretionary time at the disposal of individuals), and the rate of change in average income, together with income elasticity of demand for the particular good under consideration. Yet other conditions may be operative in the shorter run, *inter alia* the state

---

22. Disparity in growth by area is great in the United States, for example. Between 1950 and 1960 growth by state ranged between −0.7 and 5.8 percent per year; in 1960-66, between −0.6 and 7.4 percent; and in 1960-69, between −3.2 and 60.2 percent. Growth by region ranged from 0.9 percent per year in the North Central to 2.5 in the West in 1960-65 and from 0.6 percent per year in the Northeast to 1.5 in the West in 1965-68. The annual rate of growth of households ranged, in 1950-68, between 3.4 percent in the West and 1.7 percent in the North Central region, and in 1960-66, between 2.5 percent in the West and 1.0 percent in the North Central region. The corresponding expected rates for the period 1965-75 are 31.2 percent and 13.3 percent. See Bureau of the Census, *Current Population Reports*, Series P-25, No. 396, July 11, 1968, and No. 387, February 20, 1968. Intercounty and intercity growth rates differ even more widely. See also C. L. Beale, "Natural Decrease of Population: The Current and Prospective Status of an Emergent American Phenomenon," *Demography* 6 (May, 1969): 91-100.

of inventories of goods, the need to become habituated to goods new to the consumer, and the level of per capita real income (with which sensitivity to price is inversely related). The rate of increase in demand for any particular product will be affected very little if at all by population growth unless the elasticity of demand for this product is negligible; ordinarily it will depend in greater measure upon increase in per capita income.

Experience bears out our inference that the rates of growth of demand for specific products are not closely linked to the rate of population growth. For example, between 1955 and 1965, when employment levels were similar, Gross National Product increased about 3 1/2 percent per year; output per member of the civilian labor force, just over 2 percent; and membership in the civilian labor force, just over 1 3/8 percent compared with a rate of population growth of about 1 5/8 percent. Accordingly, supposing income elasticity of demand for most specific products to lie between just below 1/2 and just over 2, the rate of growth of aggregate demand for specific products might have been expected to fall mainly within a range of 2 to 5 1/2 percent. The actual range was much wider, even as in 1948-65 when population was growing about 1 3/4 percent per year, and Gross National Product per capita, about 2 percent per year. Then the average annual rate of growth of output (which approximated demand) of selected products and services ranged from over 25 percent to -15 percent and even less. Meanwhile, the demand for services of all sorts rose enough to supply most of the increase in employment recorded in 1948-65.[23] The width of this range of rates is the result mainly of changes in tastes and technology rather than of changes in income and population. Technological change introduces new products and displaces old ones. Tastes adjust to technology, and change for other reasons as well. Moreover, in an age of discretionary time and income, most people have some time and income which they can dispose of in any way that suits them. Under these conditions tastes are volatile and hence highly responsive to newly created opportunities to spend.[24]

In view of the statistical evidence regarding the behavior of demand for specific, individual products, and the importance of technological change, rising discretionary income, and changing

---

23. Francis L. Hort, "Patterns of Output Growth," *Survey of Current Business* 46 (November, 1966): 18-25; also my "Services and the Future of the American Economy," *South Atlantic Quarterly* 46 (Winter, 1967): 105-15.

24. E.g., see Lewis Schipper, *Consumer Discretionary Behavior* (Amsterdam: North Holland Publishing Co., 1964); also unsigned, "The Great Rush for New Products," *Time* (October 24, 1969): 92-93.

tastes, most business firms serving national markets are unlikely to attach major importance to population growth as a source of increase in demand. A firm will rely upon rising per capita income and its own capacity to supply better or novel goods and services, hopeful also that population growth is not multiplying its competitors. The exceptions will consist in business firms supplying only or mainly products the individual income-elasticity of demand for which is very low. Few firms answer closely to this description, now that trademarks increase 5 percent per year and about 10,000 "new" package-goods items alone are introduced annually.

This argument is less valid for firms serving regional or localized markets. For in general, the smaller a regional or a local town or small-city market, the higher may be its net immigration rate and hence its population growth rate. Here, however, we are dealing with the redistribution of population in space rather than with the rate of growth of a nation's population. While the magnitude of the redistribution movement is greatly affected by the rate of population growth, the direction of movement usually is dominated by economic factors.

Let us categorize these specific, individual goods and services, placing in a category or set all individual items quite substitutable, one for another, with the result that substitutability and cross-elasticity of demand between members of a given set and members of some other set are very low or negligible. For example, let us assemble all makes of men's suits into a set or category, "suits"; then substitutability between members of the set will be high, much higher, as a rule, than substitutability between a particular make and (say) ten theatre tickets. Then, while the population elasticity of demand for a particular make of suit is negligible, that for suits in general may be close to 1.0, that is, the demand for suits will grow at about the same rate as the population under *ceteris paribus* conditions. Then, *over time*, the growth of consumption of any one set will tend to be insensitive to change in relative price, but sensitive to change in per capita income, perhaps sensitive to the introduction of *new categories* of products, and sensitive to population growth. The ratio of the annual increment in demand for (or consumption of) sets of non-durables (so defined) to the amount annually produced and consumed is very low, probably of the order of magnitude of 2 to 5 percent at the aggregate level. Storage and variation of inventory may modify this fraction somewhat in the short run, but not enough to affect our analysis, which relates to the longer run.

The above distinction and argument do not fit all durable products. An exception needs to be made of *individual* durable products, those with long life and the use of which often is closely linked with the movement of population through the resulting growth of households.

The response of growth of demand D for a category of goods to a change in the rate of population growth may now be described. It is necessary to suppose that D and its annual rate of growth D' are little influenced by man's tastes or preferences, by his response to price change, or by his manner of adjusting to increase in average income. Given these suppositions, let us assume that population P is stable and growing at a constant rate P' while its average income y is growing at a constant rate y'. Then, given an income elasticity of demand e for the category of goods in question, approximately

$$D' = P' + ey'$$

D' would approximate 3.4 percent per year if P', e, and y', respectively, approximated 0.015, 0.95, and 0.02.

Now suppose that fertility declines and a constant rate of population growth $P' = 0.005$ replaces $P' = 0.015$. This decline, considered alone, would cause D' to fall from 3.4 to 2.4 percent per year. However, y will increase in some measure and hence push D' above 2.4 percent. How much y' will increase depends on two concomitants of the decline in P': (a) the increase in the rate of capital formation per capita made possible by the release of resources consequent upon the decline in the rate of population growth; and (b) the productivity i of this released capital C. The value of i probably falls within a range of $0.1-0.15$, since C is not only productive per se but also helps give release to increasing returns, if present, and to technical progress embodied in new equipment and trained manpower.[25] C consists in part of inputs which otherwise would assume the shape of housing and furnishings but now assume more productive forms in industry; this shift thus tends to give something of an upward push to i.

Given constant returns and a decline of one percentage point in the true rate of natural increase, what value is assignable to C?

---

25. Private rates of return in the U.S. private domestic economy exceeded 10 percent in 1949-65 but allegedly were below those on investment in secondary and higher education. See T. W. Schultz, "Resources for Higher Education: An Economist's View," *Journal of Political Economy* 76 (1968): 336-37. The returns in the private domestic economy are from D. W. Jorgenson and Z. Griliches, "The Explanation of Productivity Change," *Review of Economic Studies* 34 (July, 1967): 268. According to Harold Barger disembodied technical change is an important source of growth in some high-income countries. "Growth in Developed Nations," *Review of Economics and Statistics* 51 (May, 1969): 143-48. Issues connected with supposed increase in returns are discussed below.

With the ratio of tangible wealth to income falling between 3 and 4 to 1.0, capital amounting to at least 3-4 percent of the national income is required to maintain the wealth-population ratio in the face of a one percent rate of population growth. This value is in keeping with John Kendrick's estimates,[26] but it does not allow for the inputs required in the reproduction, rearing, and education of children, together with the cost of unproductive wealth not already included in C. Inclusion of these costs could raise the above 3-4 percent by a factor of 0.5–0.6 or more to 4.5–6.4 or more percent.[27] Multiplying these percentages by rates of return of 10-15 percent yields a range of 0.45 to 0.96 percent to offset the one percentage point decline in D' associated with the decline in P' from 1.5 to 0.5 percent. The net decline thus falls between (1.5–0.45) and (1.0–0.96) percent, or roughly between zero and .5 percentage point.

It is doubtful if the full amount of resources released by the decline in P' from 1.5 to 0.5 percent would be devoted to income-augmenting investment. Part of it would be devoted to increase in leisure, probably uncompensated by an increase in

---

26. John Kendrick's estimates suggest that about 3.1 to 3.2 percent of G.N.P. was required to support a rate of population growth of one percent per year; this figure corresponds to something like 3.8 percent of national income. See *Productivity Trends in the United States* (N.B.E.R.) (Princeton: Princeton University Press, 1961), Table 19, p. 100. In 1969 dollars the cost of raising a child at the low-cost level for the first 18 years of life ranged from $19,360 for a rural nonfarm child in the North Central region to $25,000 for a rural nonfarm child in the West, or close to $1,000 per year and 15-17 percent of disposable family income, on an average. These costs include only estimates of outlays by the family, not outlays by governmental agencies. The average would be higher, given a "moderate-cost" or a "liberal" level of expenditure. Total costs rise as the child grows, running 35-40 percent higher in the eighteenth than in the first year. Average cost declines somewhat with family size. See Jean L. Pennock, "Cost of Raising a Child," paper presented to the Forty-Seventh Agricultural Outlook Conference, Washington, D.C., February 18, 1970; the author is with the Consumer and Food Economics Research Division, U.S.D.A., Washington, D.C. Dorothy Brady's estimates suggest that "at a given income level consumption expenditures increase at the sixth root of family size" and hence that a consumption function would be nearly one percent higher "at every point if extra dependents made a population 6 per cent larger." See Coale, ed., *Demagraphic and Economic Change in Developed Countries*, p. 354. See also A. Henderson, "The Cost of Children," *Population Studies* 3 (1949-50): 130-50; 4 (1950-51): 267-98; Stephen Enke, "The Economics of Having Children," *Policy Sciences* 1 (1970): 15-30; Jacques Henripen, *Le coût de la croissance démographique* (Montreal: Les Presses de l'Université de Montreal, 1968). On the impact of demographic factors on savings, see W. Eizenga, *Demographic Factors and Savings* (Amsterdam: North Holland Publishing Co., 1961); Neisser, "The Economics of a Stationary Population"; Harold Lydall, "The Life Cycle in Income Saving, and Asset Ownership," *Econometrica* 23 (April, 1955): 131-50; and James Tobin's discussion of the life-cycle hypothesis of F. Modigliani and others in "Life Cycle Saving and Balanced Growth," in W. Fellner et al., *Ten Economic Studies in the Tradition of Irving Fisher* (New York: Wiley, 1967), pp. 231-56. See also N. Leff, "Dependency Rates and Savings Rates," *American Economic Review* 59 (December, 1969): 886-96.

27. For estimates of educational capital alone see M. R. Colberg, *Human Capital in Southern Development, 1939-1963* (Chapel Hill: University of North Carolina Press, 1965), pp. 111-113; also T. W. Schultz, *The Economic Value of Education* (New York: Columbia University Press, 1963), pp. 50-52.

output per hour of the shorter work week resulting. Against this increase in leisure may be set the fact that the relative number of persons of productive age (say 20-69 years) will be slightly greater if a population is growing only 0.5 instead of 1.5 percent per year. Economies of scale probably are not very dissimilar in the two cases contrasted.

III. POPULATION MOVEMENTS AND DEMAND FOR CATEGORIES OF DURABLES

In this section we examine the response of the demand for durables to change in the rate of population growth. The outcome is roughly similar to that described with respect to non-durables. Because there is some difference, however, the behavior of the demand for durables is examined separately.

The demand for durables, or relatively long-lived embodiments of services, is far more subject to the acceleration principle than is that for non-durables, even those susceptible to temporary storage. For, the demand for durables, being derived from the demand for their embodied services, usually fluctuates in greater measure than does the demand for these services. Even so, the demand for durables, viewed in the aggregate, need not be greatly disturbed by variation in the rate of population growth, in part because the life span of durables is not inexorably determined but subject instead to some extension or contraction when the state of demand for the services of these durables so warrants.

The life span of a nation's wealth varies with a number of conditions, rising or falling as the life span of particular elements increases or decreases, falling with increase in purposeful obsolescence and (probably) with innovation, falling with the steady decrease in the relative importance of non-reproducible wealth, and falling (rising) as the ratio of shorter-lived wealth (e.g., consumer durables, equipment) to longer-lived wealth (e.g., construction) increases (decreases).[28] The average age of the existing stock of capital, together with the ratio of net to gross capital, falls as the rate of growth of the stock of capital rises.[29] Goldsmith has estimated the average life of total output in the United States at about seven years, thus implying that under static

---

28. On the changing composition of national wealth in the United States see R. W. Goldsmith, *The National Wealth of the United States in the Postwar Period* (N.B.E.R.) (Princeton: Princeton University Press, 1962), chap. 5 and Tables A-5 and A-6, also chap. 7 on international comparisons.
29. *Ibid.*: 18-19, 26-27.

conditions the ratio of reproducible tangible wealth to net national product is 3.5.[30] He adds that it is not likely that the average life will move out of a range of six to eight years.[31]

Change in the composition of gross and net national product should reduce the tendency of the American economy to experience internally generated disturbance, given considerable increase in the relative importance of services and perishables. In 1967 services and non-durables comprised about 70 percent of Gross National Product, with producer's durables and structures, respectively, constituting about 16.9 and 12.5 percent.[32]

The following is a simple model suited to illustrate exposition in this section. The term "capital" is used to refer to durables of all sorts and to structures; t refers to time period.

Symbols	Definition	Value in $t = 0$	Value in $t = 1$
k	Capital per head	$20,000	$20,400
P	Population	100,000	101,250
$K = kP$	Total capital	$2,000 million	$2,065.5 million
d	Lifetime of K	7.143 years	7.143 years
$Y = yP$	Total income	$500,000,000	$516,375,000
K/Y	Capital/income ratio	4	4
y	Average income	$5,000	$5,000
y'	Rate of growth of y	2 percent	2 percent
P'	Rate of growth of P	1.25 percent	1.25 percent
R	Capital replacement	$280,000,000	$289,170,000
T	Gross capital requirement	$345,500,000	$356,855,124

A nation's annual gross capital requirement T originates in three sources. First and of primary importance is capital replacement $R = K/d$; in the model it approximates $2 billion divided by 7.143, or $280 million at $t =$ O, and about $289.2 million at $t = 1$. Second is the increment in capital required to match the increment in population P in the interval between $t =$ O and $t = 1$; this is $P'K$, or 0.0125· $2 billion = $25 million. Third, is

30. "The Growth of Reproducible Wealth of the United States of America since 1870," in Simon Kuznets, ed., *Income and Wealth in the United States* (published by Bowes and Bowes, Cambridge, for the International Association for Research in Income and Wealth, 1952), pp. 297-99 and notes. The ratio of national wealth to national income is higher, of course, than 3.5, about 4 or more depending on how much non-reproducible wealth is included. It may be argued that as a society becomes more affluent, its wealth-income ratio will be pushed up by increasing investment in relatively unproductive wealth.
31. *Ibid.*: 302-3, 298-99 and note. See also Tobin, "Life Cycle Saving and Balanced Growth," pp. 253-56.
32. *Survey of Current Business* 48 (July, 1968): Table 1.4, p. 20.

the increment in capital required to maintain the capital/income ratio K/Y at 4; it approximates $(K + P'K) y'$ and, in the model, amounts to ($2 billion plus $25 million) times 0.02, or $40.5 million. Accordingly, T $[=K/d+P'K+y'(K+P'K)]$ amounts to $345.5 million (i.e., 280 + 25 + 40.5), of which $65.5 million is the increment in K between $t = 0$ and $t = 1$.

Six conclusions follow. *First*, T is dominated by $R = K/d$ and would still be if d were raised to ten years. *Second*, P' plays a minor role; if P' descended to zero and with it $P'K$ and $y'P'K$, T would be reduced by only $25.5, or just over 7 percent; and if P' rose to .0225, T would rise only by $28.56 million. *Third*, should P' decline, the effect of the decline would be partly offset by the investment C of the released resources, with the result that the decline in T might be reduced to 3-4 percent or less. *Fourth*, while changes in P' and y' do not greatly affect T in the shorter run, they dominate K and the magnitude and form of the increment ΔK[i.e., y' $(K+ P'K)$]. *Fifth*, while this model, reflecting as it does an essentially stationary-state situation, reveals the gross demand for durables to be swamped by replacement requirements, it does not allow adequately for the diffusion of accelerator effects from their initial point of origin.[33] *Sixth*, the model implies the capital-absorptive capacity of population growth to be great and hence *ceteris paribus* to be quite depressive of the rate of growth of average income y'.

The above model, by focusing upon a total economy and the hypothetical response of the aggregate demand for capital to population change, neglects the fact that the accelerator principle can prove important and disturbing in selected sectors of industry. Consider the following case, with a durable lasting ten years and producing ten units of service annually, and with the last column representing the requirement of durables as replacements and additions.

Period	Population	Services demand	Durables needed	Replacements plus additions
0	50	1,000	100	10 + 0 = 10
1	50	1,000	100	10 + 0 = 10
2a	49	980	98	10 - 2 = 8
2b	51	1,020	102	10 + 2 = 12

33. E.g., see Spengler and Duncan, eds., *Population Theory and Policy*, pp. 234-301.

With per capita consumption of services at 20 per year, the requirement of durables is limited to ten replacements. But with population (and hence demand) decreasing or increasing 2 percent, the *requirement* of durables increases (decreases) by 20 percent. The accelerator effects would be greater if only 50 instead of 100 durables were required to produce 1,000 units of service, or if a durable lasted 20 instead of ten years.

The effect of greatly lengthening the life span of structures is quite evident in the impact of changes in the rate of population growth upon housing and other structures, with 30- to 50-year lives and sensitive to changes in the rate of population growth. Assume an average lifetime of 50 years for housing units and fit this assumption into the model set down in the preceding paragraph. Requirements in periods 0 and 1 become 2; in 2a the stock is adequate; in 2b requirements are 2 + 2, an increase of 100 percent above the level found in periods 0 and 1.[34]

In the previous section it was suggested that internal migration would not significantly influence the income elasticity of demand for non-durables. It may, however, slightly increase the gross annual capital requirement T. When migration takes place some capital may be abandoned in regions of provenance before its net productivity has been exhausted. Meanwhile, capital requirements increase in the area of destination. In effect, migration may slightly reduce the value d of K. With population growing this effect is likely to be zero or negligible. Given a very low rate of population growth and considerable internal migration, however, some capital would be prematurely abandoned.

IV. POPULATION GROWTH AND RETURNS

It has been shown that savings released by decline in the rate of population growth and shifted from investment in natural increase to investment in capital per head reduces the rate at which such decline would otherwise diminish the rate at which the aggregate

---

34. A companion aspect of this phenomenon is dealt with by R. A. Gordon in "Population Growth, Housing, and the Capital Coefficient," *American Economic Review* 46 (June, 1956): 307-22. See also S. M. Livingston, "Family Formation and the Demand for Residential Construction," *Survey of Current Business* 30 (March, 1950): 8-20; Elmer Bratt, B. D. Kaplan, J. Levin, and A. Zabghir, "Construction in an Expanding Economy," *Construction Review* (September, 1961): 1-15; see also Burnham Campbell, "Evidence of Long Swings in Residential Construction: The Postwar Experience," *American Economic Review* 53 (December, 1963): 508-18; also M. Abramovitz, *Evidence of Long-Swings in Aggregate Construction Since the Civil War*, N.B.E.R. Occasional Paper 79, New York, 1962, pp. 2, 3, 131, 132; J. P. Lewis, *Business Cycles and Britain's Growth* (London: Macmillan, 1965).

demand for goods and services, together with their supply, would grow. It was assumed that age composition remained constant, or at least of negligible significance, and that returns were constant. Increase in average output was assumed to take place because of (a) increase in the amount saved per capita and (b) technical progress that continued to maintain the substitutability of capital for labor and scarce resources. It was assumed by implication that aggregate demand continued adequate to absorb growing output. It was assumed by implication that the United States economy was large enough to allow full exploitation of any economies of scale. There always exists the possibility of increasing return, though this possibility commands only limited attention because the contribution of appropriately oriented and financed technical progress is so great. However, should population growth as such be a source of increasing return as Adam Smith, Allyn Young, and Colin Clark have supposed,[35] a diminution in the rate of population growth would diminish the contribution of this increasing return and thus reduce somewhat the gain derived from greater investment in output-increasing capital.

It is doubtful, however, that population growth as such makes a net contribution via the medium of increasing return in many countries, or that it stimulates or reinforces other sources of growth enough to offset all the costs and disbenefits of population and income growth,[36] some of which may escape the statistician's net within a country and do escape it when international comparisons are undertaken.[37] Because of difficulties besetting the imputation of growth to its immediate sources and the apportioning of these sources to sources further removed,[38] economists differ respecting what share of an unexplained residual of growth is traceable to economies of scale, or increasing return

---

35. Young, extending Adam Smith's views, observed that while "increasing returns" may be present even though "population remains stationary," "under most circumstances, though not in all, the growth of population still has to be counted a factor making for a larger per capita product." See "Increasing Returns and Economic Progress," *Economic Journal* 37 (December, 1928): 536.

36. For a different conclusion see A. O. Hirschman, *The Strategy of Economic Development* (New Haven: Yale University Press, 1958), pp. 176-82, and the references he cites. On some of the costs see E. J. Mishan, *The Costs of Economic Growth* (London: Staples Press, 1967), and *Welfare Economics* (New York: Random House, 1964).

37. E.g., see D. Usher, *The Price Mechanism and the Meaning of National Income Statistics* (Oxford: Clarendon Press, 1968); Simon Kuznets, *Economic Change* (New York: Norton, 1953), pp. 145-91; R. C. O. Matthews, "Why Growth Rates Differ," *Economic Journal* 79 (June, 1969): 261-68; A. T. Peacock, "Production Functions and Population Theory," *Population Studies* 10 (1957): 298-305, esp. pp. 300-301; A. L. Levine, "Economic Science and Population Theory," *ibid.* 19 (1965-66): 139-54.

38. E.g., see F. M. Westfield, "Technical Progress and Returns to Scale," *Review of Economics and Statistics* 48 (November, 1966): 432-41; Edwin Mansfield, *The*

associated with increase in the labor force (given also that increments of labor are appropriately employed and adequately equipped with capital). It is possible, of course, that in (say) 1750-1910, when the character of economies was changing and specialization was increasing, population growth did contribute to the increase of average output, conventionally defined and measured, and yet no longer does so in advanced economies today.

Denison finds evidence of economies of scale flowing from both external and internal economies as national, regional, and local markets grow in size; but these are associated with growth of market as such; they are not traced back in part to growth of population as such, nor are the other sources of growth associated with population growth. Kuznets reasons somewhat similarly, stressing especially growth of knowledge and its ease of spread, flexibility of the economy, and venturesomeness, all of which, he believes, will be greater when a population is growing than when it is stationary.[39] Here I should note that information is not free and that the spread and adoption of new ideas must surmount many obstacles. Colin Clark points to population growth as a savior of initially erroneous investment decisions, but fails to allow for the fact that this supposed protection tends to produce an offsetting increase in misjudgment and error. Clark also describes population growth as a possible generator of enterprise-favoring windfall profits, as a factor reducing the overhead cost per capita of government, and as a contributor to Verdoorn's principle according to which product per man-hour of labor input has "tended to grow at the square root of the rate of growth of total product." Underlying this principle may be increase in specialization and greater exploitation of internal and external economies, together with a learning-curve effect, or increase in efficiency on a job as it is done more frequently. In Clark's view, therefore, population growth tends to reduce the input of capital required per unit of output and at the same time to increase the supply of savings by putting greater pressure upon individuals and countries to save and form

---

Economics of Technological Change (New York: Norton, 1968); R. M. Solow, "Investment and Technical Progress," in K. J. Arrow, S. Karlin, and P. Suppes, eds., *Mathematical Methods in the Social Sciences, 1959* (Stanford: Stanford University Press, 1960), pp. 89-90, 99; E. F. Denison, *Why Growth Rates Differ: Postwar Differences in Nine Western Countries* (Washington, D.C.: Brookings Institution, 1967), esp. chaps. 17, 21; also *The Sources of Economic Growth in the United States and the Alternatives Before Us* (Committee for Economic Development, Supplementary Paper No. 13), New York, 1962, chap. 16.

39. Simon Kuznets, *Economic Growth and Structure* (New York: Norton, 1965), pp. 123-41; also Coale, *Demographic and Economic Change in Developed Countries,* pp. 324-51.

capital.[40] Jorgenson and Griliches reach a quite different conclusion, namely, "that most of the growth in total output may be explained by growth in total input."[41]

Whether returns are increasing or not is determined in the main by optimum plant size and the ease with which full use of such plants may be attained through appropriate interplant and interindustry fits. Optimum plant need not be exogeneously determined as in the past, however; its technological base is subject to research designed to reduce optimum plant size and thereby make possible interplant and interindustry fits which presuppose a smaller rather than a larger population. Research directed toward plant miniaturization may therefore serve also to reduce the economic diseconomies currently associated with small economies.[42] Increase in output per worker may also operate to reduce optimum plant size measured in terms of number of workers required to man such plants.

A different type of argument is put forward by W. A. Eltis. He suggests that "faster growth of the labour force leads to faster technical progress, and faster growth of output per worker," but does not explain the underlying mechanism.[43] One may say that an increase in the rate of capital formation tends to increase output per unit of capital, conventionally defined, if the newest capital embodies relatively the most technical progress; then the stock of capital becomes increasingly weighted with technically superior progress-embodying types. This argument is not easily extended to population growth; for the capacity of a society to embody the most advanced technical training in the most recent additions to its labor force tends to be somewhat inversely associated with its rate of population growth.

H. V. Musham implies that population growth may be easily countervailed. He writes:

$$i = c\,(r + s)$$

---

40. *Population Growth and Land Use* (New York: Macmillan, 1967), pp. 255-68; J. P. Verdoorn, "Complementarity and Long Range Projections," *Econometrica* 24 (October, 1956): 429-50.

41. Jorgenson and Griliches, "The Explanation of Productivity Change," p. 272. But see E. F. Denison's comments on this finding in his "Some Major Issues in Productivity Analysis: An Examination of Estimates by Jorgenson and Griliches," *Survey of Current Business* 49 (May, 1969), Part II: 1-27. See also Horace Belshaw, *Population Growth and Levels of Consumption* (New York: George Allen and Unwin, 1956), pp. 45-50 and chaps. 5, 11.

42. The importance of optimum plant size, commonly overlooked, is stressed in *ibid.*: 74-76, 88.

43. W. A. Eltis, *Economic Growth* (London: Hutchinson, 1966), p. 19.

where c denotes capital-output ratio; r, the rate of population growth; and s, the rate of growth per capita income if i is the fraction of the national product saved. Assume two countries, in one of which r'' is 3 percent, in the other of which r' is 2 percent, and postulate values of 2 percent for s and 4 for c. Then 20 percent, the amount of saving required to yield a 2 percent per year rate of income growth when $r'' = 0.03$ exceeds by four percentage points the amount of saving (i.e., 16 percent) required when r' is only 0.02. The level of living—output minus savings—will be higher in the latter country than in the former, that is 84 instead of 80. Moreover, given $c = 4$, a stepping up of savings by eight percentage points for each of two years in the country with population growth rate r'' would bring its level of living up to that of the country with the lower population growth rate r'. Musham underestimates the difficulty of stepping up saving in a country with a high rate of population growth and fails to take into account the fact that, even with a marginal return of 15 percent on capital, increase of s by one percentage point would call for extra savings of 6.67 instead of 4 percent.[44] Indeed, one may argue that in less developed countries there tends to be an inverse relation between the rate of population growth and the rate of increase in per capita income and savings.[45]

In what follows I shall assume that constant returns prevail in economies as wholes, other than resource-rich underdeveloped regions, and that therefore the behavior of output per capita income y is independent of the forces included under increasing and decreasing returns. Such effects as are associated with Verdoorn's principle involve two kinds of interpretative problems, determination of whether increasing output per man hour is a cause or an effect of increasing total output, and unambiguous determination of the mechanisms that might underlie the Verdoorn principle.[46] Over a long period of time diminishing re-

---

44. H. V. Musham, "Critique of Two Theories on the Population Factor in Economic Growth of Developing Countries," in Egon Szabody, ed., *World Views of Population Problems* (Budapest: Akademia Kiadó, 1968), pp. 219-29.

45. E.g., see A. J. Coale and E. M. Hoover, *Population Growth and Economic Development in Low-Income Countries* (Princeton: Princeton University Press, 1958); E. M. Hoover and M. Perlman, "Measuring the Effects of Population Control on Economic Development: A Case Study of Pakistan," *Pakistan Development Review* 6 (1966): 545-66; P. Newman and R. H. Allen, *Population Growth Rates and Economic Development in Nicaragua* (Washington, D.C.: Robert R. Nathan Associates, 1967).

46. See J. M. Katz, " 'Verdoorn Effects,' Returns to Scale, and the Elasticity of Factor Substitution," *Economica* 20 (November, 1968): 342-52. On scale economies see also W. E. G. Salter, *Productivity and Technical Changes*, 2d ed. (Cambridge: Cambridge University Press, 1966), chap. 10; Belshaw, *Population Growth and Levels of Consumption*, chap. 5.

turns in agriculture or other environment-bound activities may partly offset non-demographic forces making for increase in average output, and so may increase in the relative importance of services, the output of which is less subject to progress than that of goods. Limits to consumption may also limit incentive to produce, as is pointed out later. Constraints, which are present in man's environment and restrictive of the growth of his welfare defined to include leisure and all other relevant factors, may also limit human effort. Population growth, even though favorable to the growth of average output in a whole economy for a period, or in sections of it for a much longer time, could in the end serve as a drag upon the upward movement of average output. Though Kuznets' studies show a degree of correlation between the rate of growth of average output and that of population in a number of countries, mostly developed, the association is not clearcut, being smothered by other factors.[47] The assumption of constant returns, even should it be slightly invalid, does not affect the mode of our early argument and only slightly reduces its empirical acceptability. The capital cost of population growth in most underdeveloped countries is so high as to smother any gain to be had from increasing returns.[48]

V. POPULATION COMPOSITION; TRANSITION

In the preceding sections we held age composition constant by postulating stable populations and comparing them. We did this to show that the rate of growth of aggregate demand declined by less than the rate of growth of population when a less rapidly growing stable population was substituted for a more rapidly growing stable population. We did not, however, deal with the changes in age composition that accompany a decline in the rate of growth of a population as it is in *transit* from a stable form associated with a higher G.R.R. to one associated with a lower G.R.R. In this

---

47. "Quantitative Aspects of the Economic Growth of Nations," Part I, *Economic Development and Cultural Change* 5 (1) (October, 1956): 28-31, also Tables 1-3.
48. G. C. Zaidan estimates the resources absorbed by population growth in India at about 5.1 billion dollars at 1964 prices, or about four-fifths of India's annual budget. "Population Growth and Economic Development," *Finance and Development* 6 (March, 1969): 8. India's proposed budget for 1969-70, $6.64 billion, was 3.6 percent above that for 1968-69, according to *International Financial News Survey* (March 21, 1969): 81. See also on the economic advantage to be had from low fertility, Coale and Hoover, *Population Growth and Economic Development in Low-Income Countries*, pp. 273-75, and Stephen Enke, "The Economics of Having Children," pp. 15-30.

section we shall deal with such a change—a change that is quite smooth and regular unless the rate of growth declines precipitately, or the initial age structure is irregular. Such irregularity characterizes the age structure of the population of the United States; for in it are embedded echoes of past irregularities that had their origin in irregularities in both the net inflow of immigrants and the behavior of natural increase.[49]

Changes in age structure are accompanied by four types of economic effects besides those associated with a decline in the rate of population growth as such.[50] (1) The growth of the labor force will be affected and this in turn may produce other effects. (2) The flow of savings may change and with it, (3) the pattern of investment. (4) The structure of aggregate consumption will change since the consumption of a variety of goods and services is correlated more highly with some age groups than with others. We shall examine these effects in this section.

How important these effects will prove to be turns on how flexible an economy is and how multi-purposed and mobile are the factors of production. Optimal use of the flow of inputs depends upon how appropriately an economy responds to the four sets of effects identified above. In essence the productive or supply structure of an economy must adjust to changes in the structure of demand issuing from change in age composition. Such adjustment should prove easy if, as is usually true, most inputs or factors of production have a number of uses and can be easily shunted from one set of activities to another.

Before I deal specifically with the four effects of change in age composition, it may prove useful to deal with the thesis that a kind of demographic-economic cobweb movement will keep irregularities embedded in the age structure. Should this prove to be the case, adjustment of the economy to a low-growth-rate basis would prove less easy than if the irregularities disappeared.

According to this thesis echo effects are embedded in the age structure of the population of the United States as a result of past variations in net immigration, fertility, and the presence of 15-25 year swings in the growth of population, output, investment, and some related phenomena. These swings were associated with

---

49. Frejka, "Reflections on the Demographic Conditions Needed to Establish a U.S. Stationary Population Growth."
50. Eizenga, *Demographic Factors and Savings;* M. H. David, *Family Composition and Consumption* (Amsterdam: North Holland, 1962); E. Kleiman, "Age Composition, Size of Households, and Interpretation of Per Capita Income," *Economic Development and Cultural Change* 15 (1966): 37-58; Sidney Goldstein, "The Aged Segment of the Market, 1950 and 1960," *Journal of Marketing* 32 (April, 1968): 62-68.

variation in immigation which affected or conditioned the rate both of population growth and of economic growth, together with such indicators as the scarcity of capital (of which the supply at times was quite inadequate).[51] For, so long as immigrants were free to enter the United States in numbers that were large absolutely and in relation to the American labor force, this inflow could cushion variations in the intensity of the demand for labor within the United States even as it did in pre-1939 France and in other immigrant-receiving lands. As the intensity of resource use increased and with it the tightness of the American labor market, more and more immigrants were drawn into the American economy. They thus allegedly prevented increase in the relative scarcity of native American labor, together with sharp rises in employment opportunities and wages, from generating periodic upsurges in native marriages, natality, and natural increase. With the halting of variable but heavy immigration in the early 1920's, however, variation in the intensity of the American demand for labor, now no longer cushioned by compensating influxes of foreign labor, tended to affect this country's domestic labor force.

A result of this shift of the incidence of variable demand to the native labor force, some believe, has been increase in the variability of fertility. The amount of domestic labor entering the market could not vary in the same degree as the swings in the demand for labor, since these could be fed only by the unemployed, by earlier entry of males and females into the labor force, by the temporary recruitment of women, and by inducing potential retirees to postpone retirement until the temporary upsurge in demand had eased. Most affected, favorably or unfavorably, would be those on the verge of entering the labor market and somewhat later forming families. As a result the marriage rate, natality, and natural increase will vary much more than formerly, in sympathy with variation in employment opportunities for young Americans. Variation in the rate of population growth therefore will persist, now a result of variation in natural increase instead of variation in immigration, the demographic source of the now defunct Kuznets long swing.[52]

---

51. On the swings see Kuznets, *Capital in the American Economy*, chap. 7; Abramovitz, *Evidence of Long-Swings in Aggregate Construction;* and on the "echo principle," Jan Tinbergen and J. J. Polak, *The Dynamics of Business Cycles* (Chicago: University of Chicago Press, 1950), pp. 157, 178, 202. In the past wars, too, have produced demographic "echo" effects. See United Nations, *The Concept of a Stable Population* (Population Study 39), (New York: United Nations, 1968), pp. 3-9.

52. On the long swing see Abramovitz, *Evidence of Long-Swings in Aggregate Construction,* especially pp. 2-3, 131-32, and on its demise, Abramovitz' "The Passing of the Kuznets Cycle," *Economica* 35 (November, 1968): 349-67, especially pp. 362-63.

Two suppositions underly this analysis. The first is that variation in American fertility is dominated by variation in employment opportunities, especially in employment opportunities for the young. This supposition is not well borne out, as Alan Sweezy has shown, by American experience; for variation in employment opportunities and economic prosperity is only one of a number of variables that have affected fertility in the United States.[53] The second supposition is that the potential and actual supply of labor in the aggregate is sufficiently less variable than the demand for it to give rise to notable variation in the set of opportunities confronting young people entering the labor force for the first time.

Professor Easterlin has developed most persuasively the argument for variability in American natural increase along the lines suggested. He argues that, since an interval of about 20 years separates an upsurge of births from its sequel, an upsurge of persons newly entering the labor market, a cobweb-like relation is developing between the behavior of fertility and the behavior of the employment prospect confronting young people entering into the labor market. For, 20 years after a natality upsurge, there is an upsurge in the relative number of young people entering the labor market and this in turn produces an upsurge in unemployment, since employment opportunities do not rise fast enough. As a result of this unemployment there is a drop in natality; consequently, 20 years later the young people newly entering the labor market, being relatively fewer in number compared with available employment opportunities, may marry earlier. If they do so, two decades thereafter natality should tend to rise, as it did after World War II, when employment opportunities for the young were relatively good. "One might imagine a more or less self-generating mechanism, by which in one period a decline in the rate of labor-market entry causes a concurrent rise in the rate of change in fertility, and this in turn leads, with a lag of around two decades, to a rise in the rate of change of fertility."[54]

---

53. See Alan Sweezy's paper, "The Economic Explanation of Fertility Changes in the United States," presented at the Western Economic Association meeting at Davis, California, August, 1970.

54. Richard Easterlin, "On the Relation of Economic Factors to Recent and Projected Fertility Changes," *Demography* 3 (1) (1966): 131-53, and *The American Baby Boom in Historical Perspective*, N.B.E.R. Occasional Paper 79, New York, 1962, especially p. 32; and *Population Labor Force, and Long Swings in Economic Growth* (New York: Columbia University Press, 1968). See also Morris Silver, "Births, Marriages, and Business Cycles in the United States," *Journal of Political Economy* 73 (June, 1965): 237-55; E. Kalachek, "Determinants of Teenage Employment," *Journal of Human Resources* 4 (1969): pp. 3-21. On some economic effects of immigration, see M. W. Reder, "The Economic Consequences of Increased Immigration," *Review of*

This mechanism is bound to run down. As Sweezy has shown, there is not the close relation between variation in natality and employment opportunities for the young that Easterlin postulates. Even if there were, the mechanism would run down. As men's anticipations change, cobweb patterns become convergent. Echo effects tend to become spread out and hence to die out. Compensatory action can be taken in that women and an increasingly large number of retirees can be drawn upon to fill employment opportunities unfilled because of a past depression of natality and natural increase. According to the 1960 census, for each 100 males in the labor force, there were about 14 who had withdrawn from the labor force in the preceding decade. This figure affords a measure of the labor reserve as does the percentage of those 65 and older, reported in Table 1.[55] There we see that a possible index (see line e) of the relative importance of new entries—those aged 15-24 divided by those aged 25-64—having declined about one-fourth between 1930 and 1950-60, will increase about three-eighths between 1960 and 1970-80, and then decline about one-fifth. The relative number of new entries may then be quite large for more than a decade (even as around 1930), with the possible result that, as Easterlin supposes, marriage may be deferred and family formation delayed and checked. Not until around 1990, given the data in the table, would the ratio of opportunities to new entries improve notably. Still, returning to the labor force one-fifth of those aged 65 and over around 1970 and 1980 would slightly reduce the degree of decline between 1970 and 1990. The tightness of the labor market might be eased much more, however, by drawing on the female population aged 20-64, less than half of whom are likely to be employed, and by resorting to overtime which will be in greater potential supply since the workday and week will be shorter than it is now. Should all these steps be taken, an upsurge in natality around 1990 would be much less probable, on Easterlin's assumption, and so would an upsurge of new entries two decades later. In sum, the cobweb may be close to death by the early twenty-first century, though completion of its elimination may take longer.[56]

Economics and Statistics 45 (August, 1963): 221-30; also B. M. Fleisher, "Some Economic Aspects of Puerto Rican Migration to the United States," *ibid.*: 245-53.

55. Sidney Goldstein, "Socio-Economic and Migration Differentials Between the Aged in the Labor Force and in the Labor Reserve," *The Gerontologist* 7 (March, 1967): 31-41. Most of the data in Table I are based upon the Series C projections of the Bureau of the Census, but those in parenthesis are based on projection D. See also A. J. Jaffe and Joseph Froomkin, *Technology and Jobs*, for data by industry.

56. Cf. A. B. Atkinson, "The Timescale of Economic Models: How Long Is the Long Run?", *Review of Economic Studies* 36 (April, 1969): 137-52.

TABLE 1

Age Composition, 1930-1990

Age	1930	1950	1960	1970	1980	1990
a) Under 15	29.4	26.9	31.1	29.1(28.7)	27.5(25.1)	29.1(26.6)
b) 15-24	18.3	14.7	13.4	17.7(17.7)	17.8(18.4)	15.2(14.5)
c) 25-64	46.9	50.3	46.3	43.8(44.0)	44.9(46.4)	45.8(48.4)
d) 64 and over	5.4	8.1	9.2	9.4(9.6)	9.8(10.1)	9.9(10.5)
e) b/c	0.39	2.292	0.29	0.4(0.4)	0.4(0.4)	0.33(0.3)
f) .2 (d/c)	0.023	0.032	0.04	0.045(0.044)	0.044(0.044)	0.043(0.043)

SOURCE: See note 55. Data in parentheses are based upon Projection D.

Several or more decades must pass before the echoes embedded in the nation's age structure disappear. These reflect not only the past impact of immigration but also the decline in the birth rate to below 20 in the 1930's, together with its subsequent rise to nearly 25 in 1947-59; for the number of births rose from 2.4 million in 1935-39 to 4.2 million in 1955-59, then descended to below 3.5 million by the late 1960's. Hence, even should the average number of children per woman decline to 2.11, but with immigration continuing at 400,000 per year, births will approximate 4.1–4.2 millions in the 1980's and children under one year of age, 4 million or slightly more in 1980-2020. Should completed fertility approximate 2.45 per woman, births will average over 4.5 million in the 1980's and over 5 million after the turn of the century. Whatever the level of fertility per woman, it will rise as a result of the upsurge in females 20-29 years old in the 1970's and 1980's.

How the American population may move to a stationary level has been conjecturally projected in several studies. One such projection, Frejka's, suggests that demographic echoes would nearly disappear. He supposes the Net Reproduction Rate (i.e., the N.R.R.) to decline to 1.0 over a 25-year period, between 1965 and 1990. The population, of course, continues to grow slowly until 2060 when it becomes stationary at a level 67.1 percent above the initial level as of 1965. In Table 2 I report his data relating to the initial, intermediate, and final age structures of the female population.

TABLE 2

Female Age Composition, 1965-2060

Age	1965	1990	2060
0-14	29.88	25.52	19.12
15-19	8.47	8.17	6.37
20-24	6.87	7.62	6.39
25-64	44.48	46.72	49.57
65-69	3.47	4.04	5.19
70 and over	6.83	7.92	13.35

The population under 20 declines from 38.4 percent in 1965 to 33.7 in 1990 and 25.49 in 2060. The fraction aged 20-29 rises from 54.8 percent in 1965 to 58.4 in 1990 and 62.2 in 2060. The ratio of those potentially of working age (i.e., 15-24) to those 25-69 declines from 0.32 to 0.31 in 1990 and 0.23 in 2060. The transition depicted in this table is smooth whereas one based upon the virtually impossible objective of an immediately stationary population is erratic and disordered.[57]

In Table 3[58] are presented three population projections. The column headed D is based upon the supposition of an ultimate completed fertility rate of 2.45 per woman, together with 400,000 immigrants per year; that headed E is based upon a replacement rate of 2.11, together with immigration of 400,000 per year as in Projection D. The column headed X is based upon the replacement rate of 2.11 as in E, but with zero immigration; it terminates in a stationary population in 2037 by which time natality has moved downward into balance with a slightly increased mortality. Reference to this table is made below. Here it is to be noted that the populations described in Table 3 will not assume stable or roughly stable form until in the early twenty-first century. The trend is suggested by changes in the proportions of the population in major age groups (see Table 4).

1. Turning now to the four effects of changes in age structure mentioned earlier, it is evident from Table 3 that maintenance of interoccupational balance will become more dependent upon interoccupational migration than in the past. Thus, whereas in 1969-70 the ratio of those aged 15-19 to those aged 20-64 was 0.176, by 2020 it will have fallen to 0.131, 0.118, and 0.116 in the D, E, and X populations, respectively. There will be relatively fewer young people to man relatively expanding occupational categories, and hence more need for those in relatively shrinking occupational categories to move there. I refer to this again in the next section. It may be remarked here, however, that recruitment of an industrial or occupational category by attracting workers already employed otherwise generates more upward pressure against wage levels than does recruitment of those entering the labor force for the first time. Accordingly, should dynamic changes in occupational structure characterize the future, upward wage pressure and (probably) inflation of the sort therewith

---

57. Frejka, "Reflections on the Demographic Conditions Needed to Establish a U.S. Stationary Population Growth," especially pp. 384, 389; the table is derived from that on p. 390.

58. On the projections see U.S. Bureau of the Census, *Current Population Reports,* Series P-25, No. 388, March 14, 1968, pp. 14-16, 62-63, and No. 448, August 6, 1970. Projection D assumes an average number of 2.45 children per woman; the replacement average is 2.11.

TABLE 3

Projected Population, 1970-2037
(millions)

Age group	1969-70 Base year	1990 D	1990 E	1990 X	2000 D	2000 E	2000 X	2020 D	2020 E	2020 X	2037 X
0-9	38.8	45.8	40.8	38.9	47.0	39.9	36.7	55.4	42.2	37.6	37.3
10-14	20.5	20.6	19.4	18.5	23.7	20.0	19.3	26.1	21.0	18.8	18.4
15-19	18.6	18.6	17.9	17.0	22.7	20.7	19.4	24.8	20.6	18.4	18.5
0-19	77.9	85.0	78.1	74.4	93.4	80.6	75.4	106.3	83.8	74.7	74.2
20-64	105.9	142.3	142.0	136.1	158.5	156.5	146.9	189.3	175.1	158.3	157.6
65-69	6.8	9.4	9.4	9.3	8.5	8.5	8.2	14.9	14.9	13.9	12.2
20-69	112.7	151.7	151.4	145.4	167.0	165.0	155.1	204.2	190.0	172.2	169.8
70 and over	12.7	18.2	18.2	17.9	20.3	20.3	19.8	25.3	25.3	23.7	31.9
Total	203.2	254.9	247.7	237.7	280.7	265.9	250.3	335.8	299.1	270.6	275.9

SOURCE: *Current Population Report*, P-25, No. 448; see my note 58.

TABLE 4

Age Structure, 1970-2020
(in percent)

Age group	1969-70 Base year	2000 D	2000 E	2000 X	2020 D	2020 E	2020 X	2037 X
0-19	38.3	33.2	30.3	30.2	31.6	28.0	27.6	27.0
20-64	52.2	56.4	58.8	58.8	56.3	58.4	58.4	57.1
20-69	55.5	59.4	62.0	62.0	60.8	63.3	63.3	61.5
70 and over	6.2	7.2	7.6	7.9	7.5	8.4	8.7	11.6

SOURCE: Derived from Table 3.

associated would be greater than in the past. Rational recruiting programs could, of course, reduce this pressure.[59]

2. That the flow of savings may be higher is suggested by both the increase in the *relative* number of persons of working age (i.e., the fraction aged 20-64 or 20-69 years as reported in Table 4) and by the fact that the average age of the labor force will be higher. These conditions suggest increase in the potential output per capita under *ceteris paribus* conditions and a higher fraction of disposable income saved.

3. There will be some reduction in the requirement of capital for population growth since each of the age structures implies a lower rate of population growth. Otherwise, change in the demand for capital, being a derived demand, will depend upon whether, on balance, the structure of demand for goods and services will be relatively more capital-absorbing in the future than now. Only input-output analysis can yield a fairly satisfactory answer. Of course, should the structure be less capital-absorbing, then (abstracting from any adjustments produced by changes in the interest rate in the demand for capital and its supply) as is suggested below, there may be more scope for development of the production and sale of collective, public, and quasi-public goods and services.[60]

4. Age-connected consumption requirements reflect changes in age composition, both directly and as a result of changes in the household-population ratio (which should increase about one-seventh in 1965-85). Since the 1940's there has been considerable variability in age structure along lines incident upon the nation's consumption patterns. In 1950-60 the number of persons under 5 increased 25 percent only to decline by about 12 percent in the next decade; meanwhile the number 5-14 years old increased 45 percent in the former decade but only 17 percent in the latter decade. Whereas the number aged 15-24 rose 7 percent in 1950-60 and 46 percent in the next decade, it is expected to rise only 19 percent in the current decade. A general picture of the movements possibly in prospect is given in Table 3. In Table 5, based on 3, are given the approximate rounded yearly rates of change for the two extreme projections reported in Table 3—those for Projections D

---

59. On related issues see N. J. Simler and A. Tella, "Labor Reserves and the Phillips Curve," *Review of Economics and Statistics* 50 (February, 1968): 32-49.
60. Cf. E. A. Thompson, "The Perfectly Competitive Production of Collective Goods," *ibid.*: 1-12.

and X. While there is considerable variation in the rates, the higher rates are found generally in the upper age groups.

TABLE 5

Population Growth, by Age Group, 1970-2020
(in percent per year)

	1970-90		1990-2000		2000-2020	
Age group	D	X	D	X	D	X
0-9	0.8	0	0.2	-0.5	0.8	0.1
10-14	*	-0.5	1.4	0.4	0.5	-0.2
15-19	0	-0.5	2.0	1.3	0.4	-0.2
20-64	1.5	1.2	1.0	0.7	0.9	0.3
65-69	1.6	1.5	-1.2	-1.2	2.8	2.7
70 and over	1.8	1.7	1.1	1.0	1.1	0.9
Total	1.1	0.8	1.1	0.5	0.9	0.4

*Negligible.

SOURCE: Based on Table 3.

Changes in age composition associated with the transition of a population to a stationary state should entail no serious economic adjustments, even given some disturbance from echo effects. Adjustment at the input level is greatly eased by the fact that few inputs are highly specialized whereas most are multipurpose and hence easily reallocable among uses. Moreover, given relatively high rates of growth in the upper age brackets of the labor force, greater attention may be given to keeping older workers engaged until near 70 and thereby sustaining both output and demand for output. It is also likely that, with a low rate of population growth and a corresponding age structure, the economy may prove less prone to trade cycles. For then the demand for buildings and other structures increases slowly, since the relative importance of *additions* to the stock of structures is low. Moreover, such increase in income per capita as is associated with reduction in the rate of population growth may intensify the demand for services and consumer durables more than that for structures. As a result, variation in *additions* to the stock of structures would diminish somewhat, and with it variations in level of activity.

Should imbalance arise between ex ante savings and investment, stabilization policy might be put into effect.[61] For example, suppose the average income is growing 2 percent per year, that full-employment offsets to savings amount to 15 percent of national income, and that the rate of population growth gradually declines from 1.5 to zero percent. Eventually, there will be released from absorption by population growth resources equal to something like 35-40 percent of the initial assumed rate of "saving" (i.e., 15 percent) as well as some additional release resulting from decline in population redistribution associated with a very low rate of population growth and the elimination of surplus agricultural population. There will be downward pressure upon the interest rate which will have some effect upon both the supply of savings and the demand for them. Even so, the shift in the demand-for-savings function may outweigh the influence of adjustments to changes in the interest rate, particularly if potential demand activated by the decline in the population growth-rate lies mainly in the area of public and quasi-public goods and of non-public collective goods. Then public and other forms of collective intervention may become necessary to activate the supply of these goods.

Emphasis must, of course, always be placed upon anticipating population changes, upon keeping the economy flexible, and upon keeping factors of production capable of serving not just one specialized purpose but a number of purposes. With provision for refresher education this should not be difficult.

VI. STATIONARY ECONOMY

A distinction needs to be made between a stationary population and a stationary economy. It does not follow that, because a population is stationary, its economy will also be stationary within some meaning of the term. Nor does it follow that because an economy is stationary, its population need be stationary.[62] Even given a stationary population, this population's economy could

---

61. J. L. Stein and K. Najatani, "Stabilization Policies in a Growing Economy," *Review of Economic Studies* 36 (April, 1969): 165-84; also A. P. Thirlwall, "Okun's Law and the Rate of Growth," *Southern Economic Journal* 36 (July, 1969): 87-89, and my "Services and the Future of the American Economy," pp. 107-8.

62. "Even with a stationary population and in the absence of new discoveries in pure or applied science there are no limits to the process of expansion except the limits beyond which demand is not elastic and returns do not increase." See Allyn Young, "Increasing Returns and Economic Progress," p. 536.

continue to expand. Moreover, given a static or stationary economy, its population might still increase, but only in a manner duplicative of that already in existence and use.[63] It may be argued that, given a stationary population, an eventual sequel will be a stationary economy, whether the population is stationary because its environmental limits have been reached, or because its requirement of goods and services has been fully attained. That is, a stationary economic state may originate in the finiteness of a population's physical environment, or in the finiteness of its own wants, though emergence of the latter limit seems unlikely within a state or economy situated in a world studded with hostile or expanding states.

At this point, therefore, before examining problems associated with the advent of a stationary population, the possibility of a stationary economy may be considered. For it is theoretically possible, given a zero rate of population growth, that the rate of growth of demand for each and all categories of goods and services descend to so low a level that replacement needs dominate most or even all markets. Let us again write

$$D' = P' + ey'$$

with D', P', and y' designating the annual rate of growth of demand, population, and average income, and with e denoting income elasticity of demand. Now suppose that a new product is innovated and variously imitated until it has been multiplied into a set of imperfectly intersubstitutable units with significant cross-elasticities of demand. Taste for the set, together with demand for it, becomes diffused throughout a population P until, given y and the price structure, something like an asymptotic limit is approached. Thereafter, supposing P' and y' to be positive initially, this limit will rise with P' and ey' until the inevitable decline of e to zero makes of P' the only limit-elevating force. Then, should P' decline to zero, gross demand would be overwhelmingly dominated by that for *replacements*, a source that would become the sole source of demand should P' descend to zero.

Whereas the diffusion of sheer satiety throughout a population would press the value of e for any particular set of intersubstitutable products down to zero, a combination of three forces could set upper limits to consumption and thus greatly accentuate the

---

63. See J. E. Meade, *The Stationary Economy* (Chicago: Aldine, 1965), and *The Growing Economy* (Chicago: Aldine, 1968).

tendency for *e* to decline even with respect to an aggregate of sets of goods and services. Man may be a pleasure machine, as Edgeworth suggested, but he is a machine of quite limited capacity; his "capacity for happiness," Emile Durkheim noted, "is very limited."[64] The first of these constraining forces consists in the physical and physiological costs of consumption which limit its rational expansion.[65] The second constraining force is the limitedness of the time essential to the carrying on of consumption, since the opportunity cost of consumption time per unit of product is part of its cost.[66] The third constraint flows from failure to develop new and distinct products and hence new wants, since continuing increase in output per capita of any given collection of goods and services carries their supply to a level at which demand for them is satiated. For example, suppose there existed only two distinct products, *A* and *B*, an individual's maximum requirement of which is necessarily limited. When this limit is reached, the addition of another product *C* that is substitutable for (say) *B* will not materially modify the quantity of inputs or output that this individual is willing to exchange for *C* and *B*, or for *A, B,* and *C*. Suppose, however, that a distinctly new product *N* is developed, one that gives off different services than *A, B,* or *C* and is not very substitutable for these. Our individual now is willing to increase his supply of work, other inputs, or output, in order to exchange them for both *N* and *A* and *B*, though not necessarily in quite the same proportions as before. It is only because inventions during the past 150 years have been sufficiently product-adding instead of merely product-replacing that output and consumption per capita of goods and services other than leisure have steadily increased.[67] Often, of course, a superior type of product is intro-

---

64. *The Division of Labor in Society* (G. Simpson, translator), (New York: Free Press, 1964), Bk. II, chap. 1, p. 235.

65. Illustrative of irrational consumption is the conspicuous waste associated with potlatch, or with lavish post-mortem display of the sort described by Evelyn Waugh in *The Loved One.* On potlatch see M. Herskovits, *Economic Anthropology* (Knopf: New York, 1952), pp. 19-20 and chap. 21, esp. pp. 476-78. Even more illustrative are such modern forms of potlatch as arms races, moon and Mars trips, worldwide "good samaritanship," and so on.

66. On the time cost of consumption see Jacob Mincer's, "Market Prices, Opportunity Costs, and Income Effects," in C. F. Christ, ed., *Measurement in Economics* (Stanford: Stanford University Press, 1963); also Juanita M. Kreps and Joseph J. Spengler, "The Leisure Component of Economic Growth," in National Commission on Technology, Automation, and Economic Progress, *The Employment Impact of Technological Change,* appendix volume II (Washington, 1966), pp. 353-97, esp. 366-80. See also S. B. Linder, *The Harried Leisure Class* (New York: Columbia University Press, 1970); Jeremy Main, "Good Living Begins at $25,000 a Year," *Fortune* (May, 1968): 159ff.

67. See my "Product-Adding Versus Product-Replacing Innovations," *Kyklos* 10 (3) (1957): 249-78.

duced, one almost unique, with the result that per capita demand for it is greatly increased. Illustrative is the motorcar which, while partly displacing rail and other transport, greatly increased the total demand for transport, or, a more recent example, aircraft, whose effects have been similar; these advances in transport have also made many goods and services more accessible to potential purchasers.

As P' and ey' decline, the fraction which demand for *replacements* constitutes of total demand for any set of products—always very high—approaches unity. Producers and sellers are then confronted with new marketing problems. If ey' approximates zero and only population growth is a source of sales in addition to replacements, selling may become non-aggressive, indeed passive, with the result that a tranquil life becomes a seller's main objective, as in a village-based economy. If P' approximates zero, the seller's options are two, or a combination thereof. He may endeavor to increase replacement demand by intensifying purposeful obsolescence and reducing the average economic lifetime of products, thereby lending support to the views of those who insist that it is in the realm of consumption rather than in that of production that primary criteria of performance must be sought.[68] The seller may also pursue with even greater vigor a course of action similar to that especially characteristic of the past 75 years, namely, develop new *types* of products which are not very substitutable for those already in use and which are relatively less subject to constraints arising from the physical and physiological costs of consumption or from a growing shortage of time per day available for additonal consumption. Efforts at product differentiation might also be intensified, though to little avail since the average requirement of any particular set of intersubstitutable products would be very limited. None of the resources suggested is likely to prove very effective despite the roseate forecast of technological developments, Methuselah-like life spans, etc., currently supplied by Madison-Avenue Publicists for the Future. Production, therefore, could be continually pressing upon consumption, with probable adverse effects upon employment. Whence alternatives besides war would be sought.

---

68. E.g., see K. E. Boulding, "The Consumption Concept in Economic Theory," *American Economic Review, Papers and Proceedings* 35 (2) (May, 1945): 1-14. See also J. E. Meade's discussion of "product glut" and "capital glut" in his *Trade and Welfare* (New York: Oxford University Press, 1955), pp. 95-101; also Linder, *The Harried Leisure Class*.

One way out would probably lie in the realm of public and quasi-public goods. The production and/or the distribution of these goods might be carried out by agencies of the state or by collectivities (e.g., foundations) which may operate somewhat free of constraints of the market. The attractiveness of the latter consists in their being less subject to the tyranny of power, a tyranny probably almost as dangerous in a consumption as in a military state.

Some years ago Boulding prophesied as follows:

> There is a persistent tendency for production to be larger than consumption plus preferred investment. There is a long-run tendency to accumulate stocks beyond what investors are willing to hold [in time of peace] .... Consumption is the most important and intractable problem of a mature capitalism.... There is no continuing future for investment; its demise may be put off for a long time by new discoveries, by wars, by the opening up of new fields, but the more investment there is, the more surely does it sign its own death warrant.... The great problem of the modern age, therefore, is how, eventually, to increase consumption to the point where full production can be maintained.[69]

Should P' and ey' fall to very low levels, as is quite possible in very advanced countries, Boulding's prophecy could be roughly realized.

VII. STATIONARY POPULATION; PROBLEMS

Given the forces generating new products and the demands made by low-income countries on those approaching a stationary stage, it is virtually impossible for an economy to become stationary. Nor is it likely that the advent of a stationary population would be a prelude to that of a stationary economy. The advent of a stationary population is expected, however, to intensify a number of problems. In this section the chief of these will be considered, namely, that of maintaining interoccupational balance, that of so adjusting the structure of output as to assure balance between ex ante savings and ex ante investment and between the output of goods and services and the demand for them, and that of supplying adequate elan, enterprise, or otherwise.

A full account of the behavioral implications of a population's being stationary ought also to treat socio-psychological properties of such a demographic state. The pressure to survive is absent from such a state since, presumably, affluence will be widely diffused throughout the population. Moreover, the need to adjust individu-

---

69. Boulding, "The Consumption Concept in Economic Theory," pp. 13-14.

ally and collectively to the pressures associated with population growth and density will be minimal. It is quite possible, therefore, that most individuals will be less happy under these conditions and that the society will be weakened vis-à-vis other societies. It may prove necessary, therefore, to reshape the value structure and the content of the welfare sought, perhaps with greater emphasis than now upon man's natural environment, upon the spuriousness of much of what passes for growth, and upon the opportunity costs and negative externalities of "affluence."

TABLE 6

Age Composition of Stationary Population

Age	Male	Female
0-14	20.00	19.16
15-19	6.64	6.38
20-64	57.42	55.93
65-69	5.15	5.42
70 and over	10.78	13.10

There is no basis for concern that average output will be lowered by the changes in age structure accompanying the advent of a stationary population. The ratio of persons of productive age to the total population will be as high in a stationary as in a growing population. Consider the following stationary population with an expectation of life at birth of 77.5 years for females and 73.9 years for males.[70] Given that the labor force consists of those aged 20-69, 62.6 percent of the males and 60.4 percent of the females are of working age. This ratio is a less than perfect measure, of course, insofar as productivity and labor-force participation vary with age, but suffices for comparison in modern societies in which the physical demands on members of the labor force are limited. In view of the actual and prospective improvement in medical knowledge and its application, labor-force participation need not decline so rapidly in the 60's as at present; for the work week is short and growing shorter and the physical demands upon members of the labor force are no longer so heavy

70. A. J. Coale and Paul Demeny, *Regional Model Life Tables and Stable Populations* (Princeton: Princeton University Press, 1966), p. 25.

as formerly. The main obstacle, besides ill health, to employment of those in age-group 65-69 is man-made, namely, the manner in which retirement systems are constructed and the establishment of easily administered guidelines by trade-union and corporate bureaucrats imposing automatic retirement at some age level, say 65, without allowing the enforced retiree the opportunity to decide if retirement is his preferred course of action.[71] Should all workers be retired at 65 instead of at 70, total output would be reduced less than 8 percent since perhaps half of those in age-group 65-69 would prefer retirement to continuing in the labor force. This loss of output is of great significance, however, in our chaotic, inflation-prone economy, for the loss will be largely at the expense of persons over 64 who, if no longer employed, are virtually certain to experience a loss of 1-3 percent per year in the real value of their retirement income. Persons over 64 who did not wish to retire could continue even though their productivity had declined below a stipulated minimum—usually much below man's average capacity—provided that the rate of remuneration were correspondingly adjusted downward.

It may be noted in passing that the greatest potential source of labor input is not the fraction of the population aged 65-69. It is (a) unemployed women and (b) the extra hours which a labor force can supply if needed; with the work week averaging close to 30 hours it can easily be extended to 40 or 45 hours if necessary, and thus made to provide roughly one-third or more additional output.

It is said that interoccupational balance is more difficult to maintain if, though population is not growing, technological change continues and leads to changes in what constitutes optimum occupational and industrial balance. Thus if a population is stationary, the relative number of persons retiring, together with those removed from the labor force by death, equals the number newly entering the labor force—say at a level of 20 per 1,000 males. Under otherwise similar conditions, given a rate of population growth of 2.2 percent per year, the number entering the labor force each year (say 34) would exceed the number departing (say 12) by 22 per 1,000 and thus contribute to the maintenance of balance, since many of those newly entering the labor force would enter expanding industries and occupations.

Given a stationary labor force, interoccupational transfers prove necessary in a technologically dynamic economy. According

---

71. See Jaffe and Froomkin, *Technology and Jobs*, chap. 11 and pp. 262ff.

to the Table of Working Life for Males in 1960, death and retirement remove about 20.7 persons per 1,000 per year; their places are filled by those who survive to initial working age—i.e., 14-33—and enter the labor force for the first time. Of course, if an occupational group is of the same age composition as the total labor force and separations are not offset by additions to the labor force as in a stationary population, the membership of this occupational group will decline at an increasing rate, about 21 per 1,000 at first, about 30 per 1,000 sixteen years later, and about 50 per 1,000 fifteen years later. Should the aggregate demand for the services of an occupational group decline no more rapidly than its membership is reduced by death and retirement, outmigration from the group is not indicated. On the other hand, if the demand for the services of an occupational group increases faster than its members can supply them, inmigration into the group is indicated.[72]

While interoccupational transfer within industry or between industries presents problems as well as a stimulating challenge to the worker transferred, transfer is more easily accomplished today than formerly. Information regarding growth patterns by occupation is much better. There is much greater provision for refresher and other forms of relevant training. Labor inputs may be less specialized than formerly, with the result that the functions or tasks of which a worker is capable range more widely and enable him to meet a larger set of occupational requirements. Barriers to meeting the requirements of jobs are not great, as a rule.[73] Both mobility and the employment of older workers tend to be higher when employment is high than when it is low, and employment should be relatively high in a less cycle-prone society of the sort to be expected when the rate of population growth is negligible.

As has been noted earlier, a major concern with the prospective advent of a stationary population has been the belief that the level of ex ante savings associated with "full employment" would exceed ex ante investment and therefore result in underemployment equilibrium. This inference was drawn from the fact that, since a large fraction of investment was and often still is devoted to the support of the growth and spread of population,

---

72. These illustrative figures are based on the model given in United Nations, *The Aging of Populations and Its Social Implications* (Population Study, No. 26), (New York: United Nations, 1956), p. 56. Tables of working life for males and females as of 1960 are given in U.S. Department of Labor, *Tomorrow's Manpower Needs*, Vol. I (B.L.S. Bulletin 1606), Washington, February, 1969, pp. 56-58.

73. E.g., see Jaffe and Froomkin, *Technology and Jobs*, chaps. 9, 15. See also L. D. Singell, "Some Private and Social Aspects of the Labor Mobility of Young Workers," *Quarterly Review of Economics and Business* 6 (1966): 19-28.

decline in the rate of population growth would cause this source of demand for investment to dry up. Distinction was not made between the kinds of investment needs associated with a stationary population and the needs associated with a population's transit from a state of positive growth to a state of zero growth. For, even though problems of adjustment might arise during a period of transition, they need not persist upon the completion of transition and the development of consumption and investment policy compatible with a zero rate of growth.

It has long been argued that, even though the aggregate volume of savings should be smaller in a stationary than in a growing population, "production, especially of durable and investment goods, will encounter great difficulties in adjusting itself to demand than it would in a growing population" and hence will be subject to greater risk.[74] H. Neisser has pointed out, however, that if the mechanisms which have balanced savings and investment at high-employment levels continue to function, savings should find employment even though population is not growing.[75]

Upon the approach of a zero rate of population growth, the rate of population redistribution in space diminishes, with the result that *ceteris paribus* the demand for new and replacement buildings and other structures diminishes. Two conditions dominate the redistribution of a country's population in space, especially rural-urban and intermetropolis and intercity population redistribution: (1) the degree to which progress in agriculture reduces the absolute number of persons required to man the agricultural sector, and (2) the overall rate of population growth. If a country's agriculture is underdeveloped and a large fraction of its population is rural, much urbanward migration is indicated. For example, suppose that 70 percent of the population lived in rural areas whereas 10 percent would suffice to meet the nation's agricultural needs; then something like 60 percent are destined to move out of rural areas and thereby treble the urban population, even given a zero rate of overall population growth. A transformation process of this magnitude would require not only an adequacy of capital and agricultural progress but also a period of 25-30 years in the course of which removal of excess rural population could be completed. If, however, a country's population is growing, the relative capacity of internally growing cities to absorb a growing rural population is reduced, with the result that the transformation process might take 50-100 years.

---

74. Hans Staudinger, "Stationary Population-Stagnant Economy," *Social Research* 6 (May, 1939): 141-53; G. Myrdal, *Population; A Problem for Democracy*.
75. Neisser, "The Economics of a Stationary Population," pp. 470-90.

Even in a population with a zero rate of growth, there would be internal migration. Changes in tastes and technology will always prompt some movement. Furthermore, in most societies there are a considerable number of persons describable as migration-prone. These individuals can perform an especially useful function in a zero-growth population by supplementing the relatively small number of mobile young persons and thereby helping to maintain an optimum distribution of the labor force in space and among industries and occupations.

Two points may be made respecting the feared impact of a decline in the rate of investment. First, in a stationary population the supply of buildings and other structures, together with demand for them, will be smaller and more easily spaced optimally in time than when a population is growing (especially irregularly); for, as a result, expectations, being relatively free of the incidence of the aleatory and the transitory, take on a stable form conducive to consumption patterns of the sort associated with what Friedman calls "permanent income."[76] Second, the conditions which today envelop an economy facing a zero rate of population growth differ from those of 30-40 years ago when the stagnation thesis was popular. Today far more information is available regarding the state of an economy, actual and prospective rates of change in its components, and the links connecting both inputs and output and the components of an economy. Moreover, the economic role of the state is much greater now than formerly, with the result that private savings may have been reduced below what they otherwise might have been and that state intervention is possible (whether or not advisable) should the pattern of production not be appropriately adjusted to that of consumption. No longer, therefore, is fertility likely to be encouraged on the ground that its elevation would stimulate employment.[77]

Given a zero rate of population growth and the corresponding age composition, two problems could arise. First, potential upward mobility is limited much as in a military establishment in the absence of war or a "sickly season." Thus, at age 45, there could still survive nearly 98 percent of the males aged 30, and at age 55, nearly 94 percent. As a result, insofar as seniority is a determinant of the allocation of positions and status, the fraction of superior positions allocated to older persons will be relatively

---

76. Milton Friedman, *A Theory of the Consumption Function* (Princeton: Princeton University Press, 1957), chap. 9.
77. *Ibid.*: 120-23; Coale, "Population Change and Demand," p. 371; also William Baumol's discussion of Coale's treatment of demand in *ibid.*, pp. 374-76.

high, and that to younger persons relatively low. In the following table I present data on age structure for three male populations: (a) with a life expectancy of 68.6 years, a female G.R.R. of 1.75, and a growth rate of 18.07 per 1,000; (b) with corresponding figures of 68.6, 1.25, and 6.22; and (c) with a life expectancy of 73.9 years and a zero rate of growth.[78] The ratios on lines 6-8—especially that on line 8—reveal the increase in the relative number

TABLE 7

Age Composition of Male Growing and Stationary Populations

Age structure	a	b	c
1) 20-69	53.51	60.23	62.57
2) 20-39	28.93	28.35	26.35
3) 40-69	24.58	31.88	36.22
4) 50-64	11.44	15.53	18.11
5) 50-69	13.99	19.44	23.26
6) (3) ÷ (1)	45.94	52.97	57.89
7) (4) ÷ (1)	21.34	25.78	28.94
8) (5) ÷ (1)	26.18	32.28	37.17

of older members of the labor force in an economy with a supposedly constant job structure; they suggest that the access of persons under 40 to preferred employment will be relatively lower in a stationary than in a growing population. Intergenerational conflict, already reflected in the preference of younger workers for greater cash income rather than for greater retirement benefits, may be intensified. This outcome may, however, be counterbalanced by restructuring remuneration so as to reduce the differentials in yield by position and thereby diminish inequality in the reward structure at least to the level at which performance and output are not adversely affected.[79] In a high-income society income differentials are deemed of less importance or utility than in a low-income society; moreover, today's income differentials are more conventional than productivity-oriented in nature. Indeed, it

---

78. I have computed (a) and (b) from Coale and Demeny, *Regional Model Life Tables and Stable Populations*, p. 212, and (c) from *ibid.*, p. 25.
79. For an earlier analysis of this problem see my "Some Effects of Changes in the Age Composition of the Labor Force," *Southern Economic Journal* 8 (October, 1941): 157-75. On the destabilizing impact of increasing youth see Herbert Moller, "Youth as a Force in the Modern World," *Comparative Studies in Society and History* 10 (April, 1968): 237-60.

is doubtful if a worker's productivity rises notably after he has spent 3-5 years in an occupation, especially in one machine- or system-paced; after all, not over one occupation in ten calls for more than a high school education, and most jobs can be mastered in a year or less. Were workers aged (say) 45-55 years guaranteed job security in their 60's, they might accept this in exchange for a reduction in the degree of correlation of wages and income with age of workers.

Second, concern has often been expressed, especially in France, that there will be too little dynamism in a stationary population in which, given a life expectancy of 70 years, there would be as many people over 60 as under 15 and hence allegedly a decline in dynamism and perhaps idiosyncrasy.[80] This view attaches too much weight to biological considerations and too little to cultural ones, particularly in a society characterized by low morbidity rates in the age range 20-70 years. Individuals vary greatly with respect to the degree and the lasting power of their creativity.[81] They vary also with respect to their Vitality Index [100 (Chronological Age ÷ Biological Age)], an index which tends to rise as man's environment, health, and therapy improve.[82] Dynamism itself is the product in large measure of the institutional arrangements established to generate science, invention, and innovation and its application. It is possible also to organize public and private managerial and administrative structures so that enough persons below 40 and 50 are components of these structures to keep them quite dynamic.

It is quite likely that the content of a people's welfare index will change as its numbers become stationary, with the result that greater emphasis will be put upon economic stability and less upon acceleration of social processes and the multiplication of products. Then some of the problems believed to be associated with a zero rate of population growth may diminish sufficiently in importance to permit their solution through usual economic adjustments; for example, there will be less need for inter-occupational mobility.

---

80. On this last point see Coale, "Should the United States Start a Campaign for Fewer Births," *Population Index* 34 (October-December, 1968): 471. Cf. Glass, *Population Policies*, p. 433 note rr. On French anti-gerontocrat legislation see "Ring Out the Old," *Time* (November 9, 1970): 78.
81. E.g., see A. R. Arasteh, *Creativity in the Life Cycle. An Annotated Bibliography* 1 (Leiden: Brill 1968), pp. 80-81.
82. On this index see my "The Economic Effects of Changes in Age Composition," in J. J. Spengler and O. D. Duncan, eds., *Demographic Analysis* (Glencoe: Free Press, 1956), pp. 497-517, esp. p. 504. Cf. Alfred Sauvy, *General Theory of Population* (New York: Basic Books, 1969), pp. 303-19.

CONCLUSION

Three problems confront a society whose population is moving toward a stationary state. The first consists in the need to even out and/or countervail any perturbations—e.g., in the growth of the labor force—that accompany the transition from a positive to a zero state of growth. This, it follows from what has been said, should not prove difficult.

Second, a society must modify its expectations. A society's expectations amount to a consensus or set of individual appraisals and responses, partly internalized and subconscious, both as to the demographic and socioeconomic parameters of that society and to the natural and man-made physical environment of that society. A society's expectations are not, therefore, unchanging. They generally correspond, much as do the expectations of individuals,[83] to the seeming range of options available, for otherwise non-tolerable instability tends to be experienced, at least until accommodating adjustments are made. We may, therefore, expect both that the expectations finally encountered in a population of zero growth will differ from those found in a society whose numbers are growing one or two or more percent per year and that, under the circumstances, this new set of expectations will be more conducive to the realization of what is deemed "welfare" than would be the displaced set.

Undoubtedly, as a society's population growth moves toward a zero level, the prevailing philosophy of change will itself undergo modification. For perhaps two centuries, if not longer, Western man has set great store by change and extolled high rates of change in particular indicators, often to the neglect of the socioeconomic costs entailed. Even though it has at times been questioned whether the rate of change in particular areas, such as invention and innovation, was too high, it has not been questioned whether change in excess of a certain rate was destabilizing and contributive to societal instability and uncompensated individual discomfort. It has become in order, therefore, to inquire into what constitutes an optimal rate of socioeconomic change in a quite isolated society and into the conditions under which such a rate is compatible with existence in diverse international networks of societies.

---

83. E.g., see René Dubos, *Man Adapting* (New Haven: Yale University Press, 1965), pp. 278-79.

Third, because of wide differences in population growth by nation, a society with a zero rate of population growth is likely to have to devote attention to security against adverse action on the part of other, growing powers. What recourses are available will therefore command considerable attention. Moreover, if they are not handled with skill, the fruits that might be had from a stationary population may be lost.

In what has gone before I have not assumed, as some quite realistic models have suggested, that so long at least as the rate of population growth is moving toward zero, the rate of growth Y' of aggregate income Y proceeds independently of the rate of population growth. This assumption rests upon the further assumption that the decline in the rate of growth of a population is offset by economically beneficial effects of the decline. Then average income y' will increase because the denominator $P(1 + P')$ declines toward a constant value for P while the numerator $Y(1 + Y')$ continues to grow at some (say) constant rate Y'. Insofar as this condition holds, or is assumed to hold, a persuasive argument in support of the gradual reduction of P' to zero may be put forward. This condition will hold only given certain related conditions. It helps, however, to illustrate advantages to be had from a stationary population.[84]

While this essay has not dealt with policy as such, it does lead to four inferences. First, much more detailed analysis than has been attempted needs to be made of impact of a declining rate of population growth upon the economy. Second, implications for the international political relations of the United States need to be explored.[85] Third, there is need for sociological analysis, of associations between rates of population and economic growth, on the one hand, and the character of a people's expectations on the other. Fourth, careful inquiry needs to be made in the realm of optimum[86] population theory, particularly with respect to whether further population growth in the United States would be advantageous on balance.

---

84. Lincoln Day calls attention to some advantages of a stationary population in his *Too Many Americans* (Boston: Houghton Mifflin, 1964), chaps. 2, 6.

85. I have dealt with this question in a minor degree in a forthcoming paper, "Population and Potential Power," scheduled to appear in a Festschrift.

86. Harold Votey, "The Optimum Population and Growth: A New Look," *Journal of Economic Theory* 1 (October, 1969): 273-90; also Hans Gaffron, "Resistance to Knowledge," *Annual Review of Plant Physiology* 20 (1969): 1-40. For different approaches to the optimum, see Sauvy, *General Theory of Population*, pp. 16-64; Meade, *Trade and Welfare*, chap. 6 and pp. 573-77.

REFERENCES

Anderson, H. "Population Size and Demand," *Southern Economic Journal* 28 (October, 1961): 182-86.

Arasteh, A. R. *Creativity in the Life Cycle. An Annotated Bibliography* (Leiden: Brill, 1968).

Atkinson, A. B. "The Timescale of Economic Models: How Long is the Long Run?", *Review of Economic Studies* 36 (April, 1969): 137-52.

Abramovitz, M. *Evidence of Long-Swings in Aggregate Construction Since the Civil War,* N.B.E.R. Occasional Paper 79, New York, 1962.

Barger, H. "Growth in Developed Nations," *Review of Economics and Statistics* 51 (May, 1969): 143-48.

Bassie, V. L. "Relationship of Population Changes to Economic Prosperity," *Current Economic Comment* 20 (May, 1958): 33-38.

Beale, C. L. "Natural Decrease of Population: The Current and Prospective Status of an Emergent American Phenomenon," *Demography* 6 (May, 1969): 91-100.

Belshaw, H. *Population Growth and Level of Consumption* (New York: George Allen and Unwin, 1956).

Boffey, P. M. "Japan: A Crowded Nation Wants to Boost Its Birthrate," *Science* 167 (February 13, 1970): 960-62.

Boulding, K. E. "The Consumption Concept in Economic Theory," *American Economic Review, Papers and Proceedings* 35 (2) (May, 1945): 1-14.

Bratt, E., B. D. Kaplan, J. Levin & A. Zabghir. "Construction in an Expanding Economy," *Construction Review* (September, 1961): 1-15.

Bumpass, L. & C. F. Westoff. "The 'Perfect Contraceptive' Population," *Science* 169 (September 18, 1970): 1177-82.

Bureau of the Census. *Current Population Reports.*

Campbell, B. "Evidence of Long Swings in Residential Construction: The Postwar Experience," *American Economic Review* 53 (December, 1963): 508-18.

Cannan, E. *Economic Scares* (London: P. S. King & Son, 1933).

Charles, E. *The Twilight of Parenthood* (New York: Norton, 1934).

Clark, C. *Population Growth and Land Use* (New York: Macmillan, 1967).

Coale, A. J. "Population Change and Demand. : . ," in Coale, ed., *Demographic and Economic Change in Developed Countries* (Princeton: Princeton University Press, 1960).

——— "Should the United States Start a Campaign for Fewer Births," *Population Index* 34 (October-December, 1968): 471.

Coale, A. J. & P. Demeny. *Regional Model Life Tables and Stable Populations* (Princeton: Princeton University Press, 1966).

Coale, A. J. & E. M. Hoover. *Population Growth and Economic Development in Low-Income Countries* (Princeton: Princeton University Press, 1958).

Cocks, E. "The Malthusian Theory in Pre-Civil War America," *Population Studies* 20 (1966-67): 343-63.

Colberg, M. R. *Human Capital in Southern Development, 1939-1963* (Chapel Hill: University of North Carolina Press, 1965).

David, M. H. *Family Composition and Consumption* (Amsterdam: North Holland Publishing Co., 1962).

Davis, J. S. *The Population Upsurge in the United States*, War-Peace Pamphlet No. 12, Stanford (Calif.) Food Research Institute, December, 1949.

Day, L. *Too Many Americans* (Boston: Houghton Mifflin, 1964).

Denison, E. F. "Some Major Issues in Productivity Analysis: An Examination of Estimates by Jorgenson and Griliches," *Survey of Current Business* 49 (May, 1969), Part II: 1-27.

——— *The Sources of Economic Growth in the United States and the Alternative Before Us* (Committee for Economic Development, Supplementary Paper No. 13), New York, 1962.

——— "Why Growth Rates Differ: Postwar Differences in Nine Western Countries" (Washington, D.C.: The Brookings Institution, 1967).

Doublet, J. "Family Allowances in France," *Population Studies* 2 (1948-49): 19-39.

Dublin, L. I. & A. J. Lotka. "On the True Rate of Natural Increase as Exemplified by the Population of the United States," *Journal of the American Statistical Association* 20 (September, 1925): 305-39.

Dubos, R. *Man Adapting* (New Haven: Yale University Press, 1965).

Durkheim, E. *The Division of Labor in Society* (G. Simpson, translator), (New York: Free Press, 1964).

Easterlin, R. "On the Relation of Economic Factors to Recent and Projected Fertility Changes," *Demography* 3 (1) (1966): 131-53.

—— *Population Labor Force, and the Long Swing in Economic Growth* (New York: Columbia University Press, 1962).

—— *The American Baby Boom in Historical Perspective*, N.B.E.R. Occasional Paper 79, New York, 1962.

Eizenga, W. *Demographic Factors and Savings* (Amsterdam: North Holland Publishing Co., 1961).

Eltis, W.A. *Economic Growth* (London: Hutchinson, 1966).

Enke, S. "The Economics of Having Children," *Policy Sciences* 1 (1970): 15-30.

Fleisher, B. M. "Some Economic Aspects of Puerto Rican Migration to the United States," *Review of Economics and Statistics* 45 (August, 1963): 245-53.

Frejka, T. "Reflections on the Demographic Conditions Needed to Establish a U.S. Stationary Population Growth," *Population Studies* 22 (November, 1968): 379-97.

Friedman, M. *A Theory of the Consumption Function* (Princeton: Princeton University Press, 1957).

Gaffron, H. "Resistance to Knowledge," *Annual Review of Plant Physiology* 20 (1969): 1-40.

Glass, D. V. *Population Policies and Movements in Europe* (Oxford: Oxford University Press, 1940).

—— *The Struggle for Population* (Oxford: Oxford University Press, 1936).

Goldsmith, R. W. "The Growth of Reproducible Wealth of the United States of America Since 1870," in S. Kuznets, ed., *Income and Wealth in the United States* (published by Bowes and Bowes, Cambridge, for the International Association for Research in Income and Wealth, 1952).

—— *The National Wealth of the United States in the Postwar Period* (N.B.E.R.) (Princeton: Princeton University Press, 1962).

Goldstein, S. "Socio-Economic and Migration Differentials Between the Aged in the Labor Force and in the Labor

Reserve," *The Gerontologist* 7 (March, 1967): 31-41.
────── "The Aged Segment of the Market, 1950 and 1960," *Journal of Marketing* 32 (April, 1968): 62-68.
Gordon, R. A. "Population Growth, Housing, and the Capital Coefficient," *American Economic Review* 46 (June, 1956): 307-22.
Hansen, A. H. "Economic Progress and Declining Population," *American Economic Review* 39 (March, 1939): 1-15.
────── *Fiscal Policy and Business Cycles* (New York: Norton, 1941).
Henderson, A. "The Cost of Children," *Population Studies* 3 (1949-50): 130-50; 4 (1950-51): 267-98.
Henripen, J. *Le cout de la croissance démographique* (Montreal: Les Presses de l'Université de Montreal, 1968).
Herskovits, M. *Economic Anthropology* (New York: Knopf, 1952).
Higgins, B. "The Theory of Increasing Unemployment," *Economic Journal* 60 (June, 1950): 255-74.
Hirschman, A. O. *The Strategy of Economic Development* (New Haven: Yale University Press, 1958).
Hogben, L. ed. *Political Arithmetic* (New York: Macmillan, 1938).
Hoover, E. M. & M. Perlman. "Measuring the Effects of Population Control on Economic Development: A Case Study of Pakistan," *Pakistan Development Review* 6 (1966): 545-66.
Hort, L. "Patterns of Output Growth," *Survey of Current Business* 46 (November, 1966): 18-25.
Houthakker, H. S. & L. D. Taylor. *Consumer Demand in the United States 1929-1970* (Cambridge: Harvard University Press, 1966).
Jaffe, A. J. & J. Froomkin. *Technology and Jobs* (New York: Praeger, 1968).
Jorgenson, D. W. & Z. Griliches. "The Explanation of Productivity Change," *Review of Economic Studies* 34 (July, 1967): 268.
Kalachek E. "Determinants of Teenage Employment," *Journal of Human Resources* 4 (1969): 3-21.
Katz, J. M. "'Verdoorn Effects,' Returns to Scale, and the Elasticity of Factor Substitution," *Economica* 20 (November, 1968):342-52.
Kelley, A. C. "Demand Patterns, Demographic Change, and Economic Growth," *Quarterly Journal of Economics* 83 (February, 1969): 110-26.
────── "Demographic Change and Economic Growth: Australia, 1861-1911," *Explorations in Entrepreneurial History* 5

(1968): 115-85.
Kendrick, J. *Productivity Trends in the United States* (N.B.E.R.) (Princeton: Princeton University Press, 1961).
Keynes, J. M. "Some Consequences of a Declining Population," *Eugenics Review* 29 (1937): 13-17.
―――― *The Economic Consequences of the Peace* (New York: Harcourt, Brace, and Howe, 1920).
Kleiman, E. "Age Composition, Size of Households, and Interpretation of a Per Capita Income," *Economic Development and Cultural Change* 15 (1966): 37-58.
Kreps, Juanita & J. J. Spengler. "The Leisure Component of Economic Growth," in National Commission on Technology, Automation, and Economic Progress, *The Employment Impact of Technological Change* II (Washington, 1966).
Kuczynski, R. R. *The Balance of Births and Deaths* (New York: Macmillan, 1928).
―――― *The Measurement of Population Growth* (New York: Oxford University Press, 1936).
Kuznets, S. *Capital in the American Economy* (Princeton: Princeton University Press, 1961).
―――― *Economic Change* (New York: Norton, 1953).
―――― *Economic Growth and Structure* (New York: Norton, 1965).
―――― "Quantitative Aspects of the Economic Growth of Nations," Part I, *Economic Development and Cultural Change* 5(1) (October, 1956): 28-31, also Tables 1-3.
Landes, D. S. *The Unbound Prometheus: Technological Change and Industrial Development in Western Europe from 1750 to the Present* (Cambridge: Cambridge University Press, 1969).
Leff, N. "Dependency Rates and Savings Rates," *American Economic Review* 59 (December, 1969): 886-96.
Levine, A. J. "Economic Science and Population Theory," *Population Studies* 19 (1965-66): 139-54.
Lewis, J. P. *Business Cycles and Britain's Growth* (London: Macmillan, 1965).
Linder, S. B. *The Harried Leisure Class* (New York: Columbia University Press, 1970).
Liu, Ben-Chich. "The Relationship Among Population, Income, and Retail Sales in SMSA's 1952-66," *Quarterly Review of Economics and Business* 10 (1970): 25-30.
Livingston, S. M. "Family Formation and the Demand for Residential Construction," *Survey of Current Business* 30 (March, 1952): 8-20.

Lydall, H. "The Life Cycle in Income, Saving, and Asset Ownership," *Econometrica* 23 (April, 1955): 131-50.

Main, J. "Good Living Begins at $25,000 a Year," *Fortune* (May, 1968): 159ff.

Malthus, T. R. *Of Population* (London, 1820).

Manpower Requirements for National Objectives in the 1970's, prepared for the U.S. Dept. of Labor Manpower Administration, by Leonard A. Lecht of the Center for Priority Analysis, National Planning Association, Washington, D.C., February, 1968.

Mansfield, E. *The Economics of Technological Change* (New York: Norton, 1968).

Matthews, R. C. O. "Why Growth Rates Differ," *Economic Journal* 79 (June, 1969): 261-68.

Mayer, L. A. "New Questions About the U.S. Population," *Fortune* (February, 1971): 80ff.

——— "Why the U.S. Population Isn't Exploding," *Fortune* (April, 1967): 188ff.

Meade, J. E. "Population Explosion, the Standard of Living and Social Conflict," *Economic Journal* 73 (June, 1967): 233-55.

——— *The Stationary Economy* (Chicago: Aldine, 1965).

——— *Trade and Welfare* (New York: Oxford University Press, 1955).

Mincer, J. "Market Prices, Opportunity Costs, and Income Effects," in C. F. Christ, ed., *Measurement in Economics* (Stanford: Stanford University Press, 1963).

Mishan, E. J. *The Costs of Economic Growth* (London: Staples Press, 1967).

——— *Welfare Economics* (New York: Random House, 1964).

Moller, H. "Youth as a Force in the Modern World," *Comparative Studies in Society and History* 10 (April, 1968): 237-60.

Moulton, H. G. *Income and Economic Progress* (Washington, D.C.: The Brookings Institution, 1935).

Musham, H. V. "Critique of Two Theories on the Population Factor in Economic Growth of Developing Countries," in Egon Szabody, ed., *World Views of Population Problems* (Budapest: Akademia Kiadó, 1968).

Myrdal, Alva. *Nations and Family* (New York: Harper & Brothers, 1943).

Myrdal, G. *Population; A Problem for Democracy* (Cambridge: Harvard University Press, 1940).

Neisser, H. "The Economics of a Stationary Population," *Social Research* 11 (November, 1944): 470-90.

Newman, P. & R. H. Allen. *Population Growth Rates and Economic Development in Nicaragua* (Washington, D.C.: Robert R. Nathan Associates, 1967).

Peacock, A. T. "Production Functions and Popularity Theory," *Population Studies* 10 (1957): 298-305.

Pennock, Jean L. "Cost of Raising a Child," paper presented to the Forty-Seventh Agricultural Outlook Conference, Washington, D.C., February 18, 1970.

Peterson, J. M. & C. T. Stewart, Jr. *Employment Effects of Minimum Wage Rates* (Washington, D.C.: American Enterprise Institute, 1969).

Reddaway, W. B. *The Economics of a Declining Population* (London: George Allen and Unwin, 1939).

Reder, M. W. "The Economic Consequences of Increased Immigration," *Review of Economics and Statistics* 45 (August, 1963): 221-30.

——— "Ring Out the Old," *Time* (November 9, 1970): 78.

Robbins, L. "Notes on Some Probable Consequences of the Advent of a Stationary Population in Great Britain," *Economica* 9 (April, 1929): 71-82.

Robinson, W. C. "Money, Population, and Economic Change in Late Medieval Europe," *Economic History Review* 12 (August, 1959): 63-82.

Salter, W. E. G. *Productivity and Technical Changes,* 2d ed. (Cambridge: Cambridge University Press, 1966).

Sauvy, A., *General Theory of Population* (New York: Basic Books, 1969).

Schipper, L. *Consumer Discretionary Behavior* (Amsterdam: North Holland Publishing Co., 1964).

Schultz, T. W. "Resources for Higher Education: An Economist's View," *Journal of Political Economy* 76 (1968): 336-37.

——— *The Economic Value of Education* (New York: Columbia University Press, 1963).

Silver, M. "Births, Marriages, and Business Cycles in the United States," *Journal of Political Economy* 73 (June, 1965): 237-55.

Simler, N. J. & A. Tella. "Labor Reserves and the Phillips Curve," *Review of Economics and Statistics* 50 (February, 1968): 32-49.

Singell, L. D. "Some Private and Social Aspects of the Labor Mobility of Young Workers," *Quarterly Review of Economics and Business* 6 (1966): 19-28.

Solow, R. M. "Investment and Technical Progress," K. J. Arrow,

S. Karlin, and P. Suppes, eds., *Mathematical Methods in the Social Sciences, 1959* (Stanford: Stanford University Press, 1960).
Spengler, J. J. *France Faces Depopulation* (Durham: Duke University Press, 1938).
────── *French Predecessors of Malthus* (Durham: Duke University Press, 1942).
────── "Mercantilist and Physiocratic Growth Theory," in B. F. Hoselitz, ed., *Theories of Economic Growth* (Glencoe: Free Press, 1938).
──────"Notes on Abortion, Birth Control, and Medical and Sociological Interpretations of the Birth Rate in Nineteenth Century America," *Marriage Hygiene* (1935-36): 43-53, 158-59, 288-300.
──────"Population and Potential Power," scheduled to appear in a Festschrift.
──────"Product-Adding Versus Product-Replacing Innovations," *Kyklos* 10 (3) (1957): 249-78.
──────"Services and the Future of the American Economy," *South Atlantic Quarterly* 66 (Winter, 1967): 105-15.
────── "Some Effects of Changes in Age Composition of the Labor Force," *Southern Economic Journal* 8 (October, 1941): 157-75.
──────"The Economic Effects of Changes in Age Composition," in J. J. Spengler and O. D. Duncan, eds., *Demographic Analysis* (Glencoe: Free Press, 1956).
────── "The Social and Economic Consequences of Cessation in Population Growth," *Proceedings of the Congresso International Per Gli Studi Sulla Popolazione* (1932), Rome, 1933, 9: 33-60.
Spengler, J. J. & O. D. Duncan, eds. *Demographic Analysis* (Glencoe: Free Press, 1956).
────── *Population Theory and Policy* (Glencoe: Free Press, 1956).
Staudinger, H. "Stationary Population–Stagnant Economy," *Social Research* 6 (May, 1939): 141-53.
Stein, J. L. & K. Najatani. "Stabilization Policies in a Growing Economy," *Review of Economic Studies* 36 (April, 1969): 165-84.
Strangeland, C. E. *Pre-Malthusian Doctrines of Population* (New York: Columbia University Press, 1904).
Survey of Current Business 48 (July, 1968): Table 1.4, p. 20.
Sweezy, A. "The Economic Explanation of Fertility Changes in the United States," presented at the Western Economic

Association Meeting in Davis, California, August, 1970.
Terborgh, *The Bogey of Economic Maturity* (Chicago: Machinery and Allied Products Institute, 1945).
"The Great Rush for New Products," *Time* (October 24, 1969): 92-93.
Thirlwall, A. P. "Okun's Law and the Rate of Growth," *Southern Economic Journal* 36 (July, 1969): 87-89.
Thompson, E. A. "The Perfectly Competitive Production of Collective Goods," *Review of Economics and Statistics* 50 (February, 1968): 1-12.
Thompson, W. & P. K. Whelpton. *Population Trends in the United States* (New York: McGraw Hill, 1933).
Tinbergen, J. & J. J. Polak. *The Dynamics of Business Cycles* (Chicago: University of Chicago Press, 1950).
Tobin, J. "Life Cycle Saving and Balanced Growth," in W. Fellner et al., *Ten Economic Studies in the Tradition of Irving Fisher* (New York: Wiley, 1967).
United Nations. *The Aging of Population and Its Economic and Social Implications* (Population Study No. 26), (New York: United Nations, 1956).
―――― *The Concept of a Stable Population* (Population Study No. 39), (New York: United Nations, 1968).
United States Department of Labor. *Tomorrow's Manpower Needs*, Vol. I (B.L.S. Bulletin 1606), Washington, February, 1969, pp. 56-58.
Usher, D. *The Price Mechanism and the Meaning of National Income Statistics* (Oxford: Clarendon Press, 1968).
Verdoorn, J. P. "Complementarity and Long Range Projections," *Econometrica* 24 (October, 1956): 429-50.
Votey, H. "The Optimum Population and Growth: A New Look," *Journal of Economic Theory* 1 (October, 1969): 273-90.
Watson, Cecily. "Birth Control and Abortion in France Since 1939," *Population Studies* 5 (1951-52): 251-86.
―――― "Housing Policy and Population Problems in France," *Population Studies* 7 (1953-54): 14-15.
―――― "Population Policy in France: Family Allowances and Other Benefits, " *Population Studies* 7 (1953-54): 263-86; 8 (1954-55): 46-73.
Westfield, F. M. "Technical Progress and Returns to Scale," *Review of Economics and Statistics* 48 (November, 1966): 432-41.
Wold, O. H. *Demand Analysis* (New York: Wiley, 1953).
Wolfe, A. B. "The Population Problem Since the World War,"

Journal of Political Economy 36 (1928): 529-59, 662-85; 37 (1929): 87-120.

Young, A. "Increasing Returns and Economic Progress," *Economic Journal* 37 (December, 1928): 536.

Zaidan, G. C. "Population Growth and Economic Development," *Finance and Development* 6 (March, 1969): 8.

Zwick, C. "Demographic Variation: Its Impact on Consumer Behavior," *Review of Economics and Statistics* 39 (November, 1957): 451-56.